Geroge Parsons Lathrop

Dreams and Days

Poems

Geroge Parsons Lathrop

Dreams and Days
Poems

ISBN/EAN: 9783744651899

Printed in Europe, USA, Canada, Australia, Japan

Cover: Foto ©Thomas Meinert / pixelio.de

More available books at **www.hansebooks.com**

DREAMS AND DAYS

POEMS

BY

GEORGE PARSONS LATHROP

New-York
CHARLES SCRIBNER'S SONS
1892

TO RÖSL

CONTENTS

I

	PAGE
STRIKE HANDS, YOUNG MEN! .	5
"O JAY!" . . .	8
THE STAR TO ITS LIGHT . .	11
"THE SUNSHINE OF THINE EYES" .	14
JESSAMINE . .	15
THE BOBOLINK . .	19
SAILOR'S SONG, RETURNING .	20
FIRST GLANCE .	23
BRIDE BROOK	24
MAY-ROSE . . .	29
THE SINGING WIRE . .	30
THE HEART OF A SONG .	33
SOUTH-WIND . .	34
THE LOVER'S YEAR . .	35
NEW WORLDS . .	36
NIGHT IN NEW YORK .	37
THE SONG-SPARROW . . .	40
I LOVED YOU, ONCE — . . .	43

vii

II

PAGE

THE BRIDE OF WAR . . . 47

A RUNE OF THE RAIN . . 57

BREAKERS 63

BLACKMOUTH, OF COLORADO 69

THE CHILD-YEAR 76

CHRISTENING 79

THANKSGIVING TURKEY 81

BEFORE THE SNOW 84

III

YOUTH TO THE POET 89

THE SWORD DHAM 91

" AT THE GOLDEN GATE " 94

CHARITY 97

HELEN AT THE LOOM 98

THE CASKET OF OPALS 103

LOVE THAT LIVES . . 116

IV

BLUEBIRD'S GREETING 121

THE VOICE OF THE VOID . . . 124

" O WHOLESOME DEATH " . . . 125

INCANTATION 126

FAMINE AND HARVEST 129

THE CHILD'S WISH GRANTED . 131

THE FLOWN SOUL 132

SUNSET AND SHORE 134

THE PHŒBE-BIRD . . . 135

A STRONG CITY 137

THREE DOVES 141

CONTENTS

V

	PAGE
ARISE, AMERICAN!	145
THE NAME OF WASHINGTON .	148
GRANT'S DIRGE . . .	150
BATTLE DAYS . .	159
KEENAN'S CHARGE . .	163
MARTHY VIRGINIA'S HAND . .	168
GETTYSBURG: A BATTLE ODE .	172
NOTES . . .	187

I

STRIKE HANDS, YOUNG MEN!

Strike hands, young men!
We know not when
Death or disaster comes,
Mightier than battle-drums
To summon us away.
Death bids us say farewell
To all we love, nor stay
For tears; — and who can tell
How soon misfortune's hand
May smite us where we stand,
Dragging us down, aloof,
Under the swift world's hoof?

Strike hands for faith, and power
To gladden the passing hour;
To wield the sword, or raise a song; —
To press the grape; or crush out wrong.
And strengthen right.

5

Give me the man of sturdy palm
And vigorous brain;
Hearty, companionable, sane,
'Mid all commotions calm,
Yet filled with quick, enthusiastic fire; —
Give me the man
Whose impulses aspire,
And all his features seem to say, " I can ! "

Strike hands, young men !
'T is yours to help rebuild the State,
And keep the Nation great.
With act and speech and pen
'T is yours to spread
The morning-red
That ushers in a grander day:
To scatter prejudice that blinds,
And hail fresh thoughts in noble minds;
To overthrow bland tyrannies
That cheat the people, and with slow disease
Change the Republic to a mockery.
Your words can teach that liberty
Means more than just to cry " We 're free "
While bending to some new-found yoke.
So shall each unjust bond be broke,

Each toiler gain his meet reward,
And life sound forth a truer chord.

Ah, if we so have striven,
And mutually the grasp have given
Of brotherhood,
To work each other and the whole race good;
What matter if the dream
Come only partly true,
And all the things accomplished seem
Feeble and few?
At least, when summer's flame burns low
And on our heads the drifting snow
Settles and stays,
We shall rejoice that in our earlier days
We boldly then
Struck hands, young men!

"O JAY!"

O jay —
Blue-jay! —
What are you trying to say?
I remember, in the spring
You pretended you could sing;
But your voice is now still queerer,
And as yet you 've come no nearer
To a song.
In fact, to sum the matter,
I never heard a flatter
Failure than your doleful clatter.
Don't you think it 's wrong?
It was sweet to hear your note,
I 'll not deny,
When April set pale clouds afloat
O'er the blue tides of sky,
And 'mid the wind's triumphant drums
You, in your white and azure coat,
A herald proud, came forth to cry,
"The royal summer comes!"

But now that autumn 's here,
And the leaves curl up in sheer
Disgust,
And the cold rains fringe the pine,
You really must
Stop that supercilious whine —
Or you 'll be shot, by some mephitic
Angry critic.

You don't fulfill your early promise :
You 're not the smartest
Kind of artist,
Any more than poor Blind Tom is.
Yet somehow, still,
There 's meaning in your screaming bill.
What *are* you trying to say ?

Sometimes your piping is delicious,
And then again it 's simply vicious;
Though on the whole the varying jangle
Weaves round me an entrancing tangle
Of memories grave or joyous:
Things to weep or laugh at;
Love that lived at a hint, or
Days so sweet, they 'd cloy us;

Nights I have spent with friends; —
Glistening groves of winter,
And the sound of vanished feet
That walked by the ripening wheat;
With other things. . . . Not the half that
Your cry familiar blends
Can I name, for it is mostly
Very ghostly; —
Such mixed-up things your voice recalls,
With its peculiar quirks and falls.

Possibly, then, your meaning, plain,
Is that your harsh and broken strain
Tallies best with a world of pain.

Well, I 'll admit
There 's merit in a voice that 's truthful:
Yours is not honey-sweet nor youthful,
But querulously fit.
And if we cannot sing, we 'll say
Something to the purpose, jay!

THE STAR TO ITS LIGHT

" Go," said the star to its light:
" Follow your fathomless flight!
    Into the dreams of space
    Carry the joy of my face.
  Go," said the star to its light:
" Tell me the tale of your flight."

  As the mandate rang
    The heavens through,
  Quick the ray sprang:
    Unheard it flew,
Sped by the touch of an unseen spur.
    It crumbled the dusk of the deep
    That folds the worlds in sleep,
And shot through night with noiseless stir.

  Then came the day;
  And all that swift array
  Of diamond-sparkles died.
  And lo! the far star cried:
" My light has lost its way!"

Ages on ages passed:
The light returned, at last.

" What have you seen,
     What have you heard —
   O ray serene,
     O flame-winged bird
   I loosed on endless air?
   Why do you look so faint and white?" —
   Said the star to its light.

" O star," said the tremulous ray,
" Grief and struggle I found.
   Horror impeded my way.
   Many a star and sun
   I passed and touched, on my round.
   Many a life undone
   I lit with a tender gleam:
   I shone in the lover's eyes,
   And soothed the maiden's dream.
   But alas for the stifling mist of lies!
   Alas, for the wrath of the battle-field
   Where my glance was mixed with blood!
   And woe for the hearts by hate congealed,
   And the crime that rolls like a flood!

Too vast is the world for me;
Too vast for the sparkling dew
Of a force like yours to renew.
Hopeless the world's immensity!
The suns go on without end:
The universe holds no friend:
And so I come back to you."

"Go," said the star to its light:
"You have not told me aright.
This you have taught: I am one
In a million of million others —
Stars, or planets, or men;—
And all of these are my brothers.
Carry that message, and then
My guerdon of praise you have won!
Say that I serve in my place:
Say I will hide my own face
Ere the sorrows of others I shun.
So, then, my trust you 'll requite.
Go!"— said the star to its light.

"THE SUNSHINE OF THINE EYES"

The sunshine of thine eyes,
  (O still, celestial beam!)
Whatever it touches it fills
  With the life of its lambent gleam.

The sunshine of thine eyes,
  O let it fall on me!
Though I be but a mote of the air,
  I could turn to gold for thee!

JESSAMINE

Here stands the great tree still, with broad bent
    head;
Its wide arms grown aweary, yet outspread
With their old blessing. But wan memory weaves
Strange garlands, now, amongst the darkening
    leaves.
           And the moon hangs low in the elm.

Beneath these glimmering arches Jessamine
Walked with her lover long ago; and in
The leaf-dimmed light he questioned, and she spoke;
Then on them both, supreme, love's radiance broke.
           And the moon hangs low in the elm.

Sweet Jessamine we called her; for she shone
Like blossoms that in sun and shade have grown,
Gathering from each alike a perfect white,
Whose rich bloom breaks opaque through darkest
    night.
           And the moon hangs low in the elm.

15

For this her sweetness Walt, her lover, sought
To win her; wooed her here, his heart o'er-
    fraught
With fragrance of her being; and gained his plea.
So " We will wed," they said, " beneath this tree."
           And the moon hangs low in the elm.

Yet dreams of conquering greater prize for her
Roused his wild spirit with a glittering spur.
Eager for wealth, far, far from home he sailed;
And life paused;—while she watched joy vanish,
    veiled.
           And the moon hangs low in the elm.

Ah, better at the elm-tree's sunbrowned feet
If he had been content to let life fleet
Its wonted way!—lord of his little farm,
In zest of joys or cares unmixed with harm.
           And the moon hangs low in the elm.

For, as against a snarling sea one steers,
He battled vainly with the surging years;
While ever Jessamine must watch and pine,
Her vision bounded by the bleak sea-line.
           And the moon hangs low in the elm.

Then silence fell; and all the neighbors said
That Walt had married, faithless, or was dead:
Unmoved in constancy, her tryst she kept,
Each night beneath the tree, ere sorrow slept.
                    And the moon hangs low in the elm.

So, circling years went by, till in her face
Slow melancholy wrought a mingled grace,
Of early joy with suffering's hard alloy —
Refined and rare, no doom could e'er destroy.
                    And the moon hangs low in the elm.

Sometimes at twilight, when sweet Jessamine
Slow-footed, weary-eyed, passed by to win
The elm, we smiled for pity of her, and mused
On love that so could live, with love refused.
                    And the moon hangs low in the elm.

And none could hope for her. But she had grown
Too high in love, for hope. She bloomed alone,
Aloft in proud devotion; and secure
Against despair; so sweet her faith, so sure.
                    And the moon hangs low in the elm.

Her wandering lover knew not well her soul.
Discouraged, on disaster's changing shoal

Stranding, he waited; starved on selfish pride,
Long years; nor would obey love's homeward tide.
            And the moon hangs low in the elm.

But, bitterly repenting of his sin,
Deeper at last he learned to look within
Sweet Jessamine's true heart—when the past, dead,
Mocked him with wasted years forever fled.
            And the moon hangs low in the elm.

Late, late, oh late, beneath the tree stood two;
In trembling joy, and wondering " Is it true?"—
Two that were each like some strange, misty wraith:
Yet each on each gazed with a living faith.
            And the moon hangs low in the elm.

Even to the tree-top sang the wedding-bell:
Even to the tree-top tolled the passing knell.
Beneath it Walt and Jessamine were wed,
Beneath it many a year has she lain dead.
            And the moon hangs low in the elm.

Here stands the great tree, still.   But age has crept
Through every coil, while Walt each night has kept
The tryst alone. Hark! with what windy might
The boughs chant o'er her grave their burial-rite!
            And the moon hangs low in the elm.

THE BOBOLINK

How sweetly sang the bobolink,
    When thou, my love, wast nigh!
His liquid music from the brink
Of some cloud-fountain seemed to sink,
    Far in the blue-domed sky.

How sadly sings the bobolink!
    No more my love is nigh:
Yet rise, my spirit, rise, and drink
Once more from that cloud-fountain's brink,—
    Once more before I die!

SAILOR'S SONG, RETURNING

The sea goes up; the sky comes down.
Oh, can you spy the ancient town,—
The granite hills so green and gray,
That rib the land behind the bay?
    O ye ho, boys. Spread her wings!
    Fair winds, boys: send her home!
        O ye ho!

Three years? Is it so long that we
Have lived upon the lonely sea?
Oh, often I thought we 'd see the town,
When the sea went up, and the sky came down.
    O ye ho, boys. Spread her wings!

Even the winter winds would rouse
A memory of my father's house;
For round his windows and his door
They made the same deep, mouthless roar.
    O ye ho, boys. Spread her wings!

20

And when the summer's breezes beat,
Methought I saw the sunny street
Where stood my Kate. Beneath her hand
She gazed far out, far out from land.
    O ye ho, boys. Spread her wings!

Farthest away, I oftenest dreamed
That I was with her. Then it seemed
A single stride the ocean wide
Had bridged, and brought me to her side.
    O ye ho, boys. Spread her wings!

But though so near we 're drawing, now,
'T is farther off—I know not how.
We sail and sail: we see no home.
Would that we into port were come!
    O ye ho, boys. Spread her wings!

At night, the same stars o'er the mast:
The mast sways round — however fast
We fly—still sways and swings around
One scanty circle's starry bound.
    O ye ho, boys. Spread her wings!

Ah, many a month those stars have shone,
And many a golden morn has flown,

Since that so solemn, happy morn,
When, I away, my babe was born.
    O ye ho, boys. Spread her wings!

And, though so near we 're drawing, now,
'T is farther off — I know not how: —
I would not aught amiss had come
To babe or mother there, at home!
    O ye ho, boys. Spread her wings!

'T is but a seeming: swiftly rush
The seas, beneath. I hear the crush
Of foamy ridges 'gainst the prow.
Longing outspeeds the breeze, I know.
    O ye ho, boys. Spread her wings!

Patience, my mates! Though not this eve
We cast our anchor, yet believe,
If but the wind holds, short the run:
We 'll sail in with to-morrow's sun.
    O ye ho, boys. Spread her wings!
    Fair winds, boys: send her home!
       O ye ho!

FIRST GLANCE

A budding mouth and warm blue eyes;
A laughing face; and laughing hair,—
    So ruddy was its rise
    From off that forehead fair;

Frank fervor in whate'er she said,
And a shy grace when she was still;
    A bright, elastic tread;
    Enthusiastic will;

These wrought the magic of a maid
As sweet and sad as the sun in spring;—
    Joyous, yet half-afraid
    Her joyousness to sing.

BRIDE BROOK

Wide as the sky Time spreads his hand,
  And blindly over us there blows
A swarm of years that fill the land,
  Then fade, and are as fallen snows.

Behold, the flakes rush thick and fast;
  Or are they years, that come between,—
When, peering back into the past,
  I search the legendary scene?

Nay. Marshaled down the open coast,
  Fearless of that low rampart's frown,
The winter's white-winged, footless host
  Beleaguers ancient Saybrook town.

And when the settlers wake they stare
  On woods half-buried, white and green,
A smothered world, an empty air:
  Never had such deep drifts been seen!

But "Snow lies light upon my heart!
   An thou," said merry Jonathan Rudd,
"Wilt wed me, winter shall depart,
   And love like spring for us shall bud."

"Nay, how," said Mary, "may that be?
   No minister nor magistrate
Is here, to join us solemnly;
   And snow-banks bar us, every gate."

"Winthrop at Pequot Harbor lies,"
   He laughed. And with the morrow's sun
He faced the deputy's dark eyes:
   "How soon, sir, may the rite be done?"

"At Saybrook? There the power 's not mine,"
   Said he. "But at the brook we 'll meet,
That ripples down the boundary line;
   There you may wed, and Heaven shall see 't."

Forth went, next day, the bridal train
   Through vistas dreamy with gray light.
The waiting woods, the open plain,
   Arrayed in consecrated white,

Received and ushered them along.
　The very beasts before them fled,
Charmed by the spell of inward song
　These lovers' hearts around them spread.

Four men with netted foot-gear shod
　Bore the maid's carrying-chair aloft;
She swayed above, as roses nod
　On the lithe stem their bloom-weight soft.

At last beside the brook they stood,
　With Winthrop and his followers;
The maid in flake-embroidered hood,
　The magistrate well cloaked in furs,

That, parting, showed a glimpse beneath
　Of ample, throat-encircling ruff
As white as some wind-gathered wreath
　Of snow quilled into plait and puff.

A few grave words, a question asked;
　Eyelids that with the answer fell
Like falling petals;— form that tasked
　Brief time;— and so was wrought the spell!

Then " Brooklet," Winthrop smiled and said,
" Frost's finger on thy lip makes dumb
The voice wherewith thou shouldst have sped
    These lovers on their way.   But, come,

" Henceforth forever be thou known
    By memory of this day's fair bride:
So shall thy slender music's moan
    Sweeter into the ocean glide!"

Then laughed they all, and sudden beams
    Of sunshine quivered through the sky.
Below the ice, the unheard stream's
    Clear heart thrilled on in ecstasy;

And lo, a visionary blush
    Stole warmly o'er the voiceless wild;
And in her rapt and wintry hush
    The lonely face of Nature smiled.

Ah, Time, what wilt thou ?   Vanished quite
    Is all that tender vision now;
And, like lost snow-flakes in the night,
    Mute are the lovers as their vow.

And O thou little, careless brook,
   Hast thou thy tender trust forgot?
Her modest memory forsook,
   Whose name, known once, thou utterest not?

Spring wakes the rill's blithe minstrelsy;
   In willow bough or alder bush
Birds sing, o'er golden filigree
   Of pebbles 'neath the flood's clear gush;

But none can tell us of that name
   More than the " Mary."   Men still say
" Bride Brook " in honor of her fame;
   But all the rest has passed away.

MAY-ROSE

[FOR A BIRTHDAY : MAY 20]

On this day to life she came —
　　May-Rose, my May-Rose!
With scented breeze, with flowered flame,
She touched the earth and took her name
　　　　Of May, Rose.

Here, to-day, she grows and flowers —
　　May-Rose, my May-Rose.
All my life with light she dowers,
And colors all the coming hours
　　　　With May, Rose!

THE SINGING WIRE

Ethereal, faint that music rang,
 As, with the bosom of the breeze,
  It rose and fell and murmuring sang
   Æolian harmonies!

I turned; again the mournful chords,
 In random rhythm lightly flung
  From off the wire, came shaped in words;
   And thus meseemed, they sung:

" I, messenger of many fates,
 Strung to the tones of woe or weal,
  Fine nerve that thrills and palpitates
   With all men know or feel,—

" Is it so strange that I should wail?
 Leave me my tearless, sad refrain,
  When in the pine-top wakes the gale
   That breathes of coming rain.

"There is a spirit in the post;
　　It, too, was once a murmuring tree;
　　　Its withered, sad, imprisoned ghost
　　　　Echoes my melody.

"Come close, and lay your listening ear
　　Against the bare and branchless wood.
　　　Can you not hear it crooning clear,
　　　　As though it understood?"

　I listened to the branchless pole
　　That held aloft the singing wire;
　　　I heard its muffled music roll,
　　　　And stirred with sweet desire:

"O wire more soft than seasoned lute,
　　Hast thou no sunlit word for me?
　　　Though long to me so coyly mute,
　　　　Her heart may speak through thee!"

　I listened, but it was in vain.
　　At first, the wind's old wayward will
　　　Drew forth the tearless, sad refrain.
　　　　That ceased; and all was still.

But suddenly some kindling shock
   Struck flashing through the wire: a bird,
      Poised on it, screamed and flew; the flock
      Rose with him; wheeled and whirred.

Then to my soul there came this sense:
   " Her heart has answered unto thine;
      She comes, to-night. Go, speed thee hence:
      " Meet her; no more repine! "

Perhaps the fancy was far-fetched;
   And yet, perhaps, it hinted true.
      Ere moonrise, Love, a hand was stretched
      In mine, that gave me — you!

And so more dear to me has grown
   Than rarest tones swept from the lyre,
      The minor movement of that moan
      In yonder singing wire.

Nor care I for the will of states,
   Or aught beside, that smites that string,
      Since then so close it knit our fates,
      What time the bird took wing!

THE HEART OF A SONG

Dear love, let this my song fly to you:
    Perchance forget it came from me.
It shall not vex you, shall not woo you;
    But in your breast lie quietly.

Only beware, when once it tarries
    I cannot coax it from you, then.
This little song my whole heart carries,
    And ne'er will bear it back again.

For if its silent passion grieve you,
    My heart would then too heavy grow;—
And it can never, never leave you,
    If joy of yours must with it go!

SOUTH-WIND

Soft-throated South, breathing of summer's ease
  (Sweet breath, whereof the violet's life is made!)
  Through lips moist-warm, as thou hadst lately
    stayed
'Mong rosebuds, wooing to the cheeks of these
Loth blushes faint and maidenly:—rich breeze,
  Still doth thy honeyed blowing bring a shade
  Of sad foreboding. In thy hand is laid
The power to build or blight the fruit of trees,
The deep, cool grass, and field of thick-combed
    grain.

Even so my Love may bring me joy or woe,
  Both measureless, but either counted gain
Since given by her. For pain and pleasure flow
  Like tides upon us of the self-same sea.
  Tears are the gems of joy and misery.

THE LOVER'S YEAR

Thou art my morning, twilight, noon, and eve,
  My summer and my winter, spring and fall;
  For Nature left on thee a touch of all
The moods that come to gladden or to grieve
  The heart of Time, with purpose to relieve
  From lagging sameness. So do these forestall
  In thee such o'erheaped sweetnesses as pall
Too swiftly, and the taster tasteless leave.

Scenes that I love to me always remain
  Beautiful, whether under summer sun
Beheld, or, storm-dark, stricken across with rain.
  So, through all humors, thou 'rt the same sweet
      one:
Doubt not I love thee well in each, who see
Thy constant change is changeful constancy.

NEW WORLDS

With my beloved I lingered late one night.
   At last the hour when I must leave her came:
   But, as I turned, a fear I could not name
Possessed me that the long sweet evening might
Prelude some sudden storm, whereby delight
   Should perish. What if death, ere dawn, should
      claim
   One of us? What, though living, not the same
Each should appear to each in morning-light?

Changed did I find her, truly, the next day:
   Ne'er could I see her as of old again.
That strange mood seemed to draw a cloud
      away,
   And let her beauty pour through every vein
Sunlight and life, part of me. Thus the lover
With each new morn a new world may discover.

NIGHT IN NEW YORK

Haunted by unknown feet —
Ways of the midnight hour!
Strangely you murmur below me,
Strange is your half-silent power.
Places of life and of death,
Numbered and named as streets,
What, through your channels of stone,
Is the tide that unweariedly beats?
A whisper, a sigh-laden breath,
Is all that I hear of its flowing.
Footsteps of stranger and foe —
Footsteps of friends, could we meet —
Alike to me in my sorrow;
Alike to a life left alone.
Yet swift as my heart they throb,
They fall thick as tears on the stone:
My spirit perchance may borrow
New strength from their eager tone.

Still ever that slip and slide
Of the feet that shuffle or glide,
And linger or haste through the populous waste
Of the shadowy, dim-lit square!
And I know not, from the sound,
As I sit and ponder within,
The goal to which those steps are bound,—
On hest of mercy, or hest of sin,
Or joy's short-measured round;
Yet a meaning deep they bear
In their vaguely muffled din.

Roar of the multitude,
Chafe of the million-crowd,
To this you are all subdued
In the murmurous, sad night-air!
Yet whether you thunder aloud,
Or hush your tone to a prayer,
You chant amain through the modern maze
The only epic of our days.

Still as death are the places of life;
The city seems crumbled and gone,
Sunk 'mid invisible deeps —
The city so lately rife
With the stir of brain and brawn.

Haply it only sleeps;
But what if indeed it were dead,
And another earth should arise
To greet the gray of the dawn?
Faint then our epic would wail
To those who should come in our stead.
But what if that earth were ours?
What if, with holier eyes,
We should meet the new hope, and not fail?

Weary, the night grows pale:
With a blush as of opening flowers
Dimly the east shines red.
Can it be that the morn shall fulfil
My dream, and refashion our clay
As the poet may fashion his rhyme?
Hark to that mingled scream
Rising from workshop and mill —
Hailing some marvelous sight;
Mighty breath of the hours,
Poured through the trumpets of steam;
Awful tornado of time,
Blowing us whither it will!

God has breathed in the nostrils of night,
And behold, it is daẏ!

THE SONG-SPARROW

Glimmers gray the leafless thicket
  Close beside my garden gate,
Where, so light, from post to picket
  Hops the sparrow, blithe, sedate;
    Who, with meekly folded wing,
    Comes to sun himself and sing.

It was there, perhaps, last year,
  That his little house he built;
For he seems to perk and peer,
  And to twitter, too, and tilt
    The bare branches in between,
    With a fond, familiar mien.

Once, I know, there was a nest,
  Held there by the sideward thrust
Of those twigs that touch his breast;
  Though 't is gone now. Some rude gust
    Caught it, over-full of snow,—
    Bent the bush,— and stole it so.

Thus our highest holds are lost,
　In the ruthless winter's wind,
When, with swift-dismantling frost,
　　The green woods we dwelt in, thinn'd
　　　Of their leafage, grow too cold
　　　For frail hopes of summer's mold.

But if we, with spring-days mellow,
　Wake to woeful wrecks of change,
And the sparrow's ritornello
　Scaling still its old sweet range ;
　　　Can we do a better thing
　　　Than, with him, still build and sing ?

Oh, my sparrow, thou dost breed
　Thought in me beyond all telling ;
Shootest through me sunlight, seed,
　And fruitful blessing, with that welling
　　　Ripple of ecstatic rest
　　　Gurgling ever from thy breast !

And thy breezy carol spurs
　Vital motion in my blood,
Such as in the sap-wood stirs,
　Swells and shapes the pointed bud

Of the lilac; and besets
The hollow thick with violets.

Yet I know not any charm
  That can make the fleeting time
Of thy sylvan, faint alarm
  Suit itself to human rhyme:
    And my yearning rhythmic word
    Does thee grievous wrong, blithe bird.

So, however thou hast wrought
  This wild joy on heart and brain,
It is better left untaught.
  Take thou up the song again:
    There is nothing sad afloat
    On the tide that swells thy throat!

I LOVED YOU, ONCE —

And did you think my heart
  Could keep its love unchanging,
Fresh as the buds that start
  In spring, nor know estranging?
Listen! The buds depart:
  I loved you once, but now —
  I love you more than ever.

'T is not the early love;
  With day and night it alters,
And onward still must move
  Like earth, that never falters
For storm or star above.
  I loved you once; but now —
  I love you more than ever.

With gifts in those glad days
  How eagerly I sought you!
Youth, shining hope, and praise:
  These were the gifts I brought you.
In this world little stays:

43

I loved you once, but now —
I love you more than ever.

A child with glorious eyes
  Here in our arms half sleeping —
So passion wakeful lies;
  Then grows to manhood, keeping
Its wistful, young surprise:
  I loved you once, but now —
  I love you more than ever.

When age's pinching air
  Strips summer's rich possession,
And leaves the branches bare,
  My secret in confession
Still thus with you I 'll share:
  I loved you once, but now —
  I love you more than ever.

II

THE BRIDE OF WAR

(ARNOLD'S MARCH TO CANADA, 1775)

I

The trumpet, with a giant sound,
　　Its harsh war-summons wildly sings;
　　And, bursting forth like mountain-springs,
Poured from the hillside camping-ground,
　　Each swift battalion shouting flings
Its force in line; where you may see
The men, broad-shouldered, heavily
Sway to the swing of the march; their heads
Dark like the stones in river-beds.

　　Lightly the autumn breezes
　　Play with the shining dust-cloud
　　Rising to the sunset rays
　　From feet of the moving column.
　　Soft, as you listen, comes
　　The echo of iterant drums,

Brought by the breezes light
From the files that follow the road.
A moment their guns have glowed
Sun-smitten : then out of sight
They suddenly sink,
Like men who touch a new grave's brink!

II

So it was the march began,
  The march of Morgan's riflemen,
Who like iron held the van
In unhappy Arnold's plan
  To win Wolfe's daring fame again.
With them, by her husband's side,
  Jemima Warner, nobly free,
Moved more fair than when, a bride,
  One year since, she strove to hide
The blush it was a joy to see.

III

O distant, terrible forests of Maine,
  With huge trees numberless as the rain
That falls on your lonely lakes!
(It falls and sings through the years, but wakes
  No answering echo of joy or pain.)

Your tangled wilderness was tracked
  With struggle and sorrow and vengeful act
'Gainst Puritan, pagan, and priest.
Where wolf and panther and serpent ceased,
  Man added the horrors your dark maze lacked.

The land was scarred with deeds not good,
  Like the fretting of worms on withered
    wood.
What if its venomous spell
Breathed into Arnold a prompting of Hell,
  With slow empoisoning force indued?

IV

As through that dreary realm he went,
  Followed a shape of dark portent: —
Pard-like, of furtive eye, with brain
  To treason narrowing, Aaron Burr,
Moved loyal-seeming in the train,
  Led by the arch-conspirator.
And craven Enos closed the rear,
Whose honor's flame died out in fear.
Not sooner does the dry bough burn
And into fruitless ashes turn,

Than he with whispered, false command
Drew back the hundreds in his hand;
Fled like a shade; and all forsook.

Wherever Arnold bent his look,
Danger and doubt around him hung;
And pale Disaster, shrouded, flung
Black omens in his track, as though
The fingers of a future woe
Already clutched his life, to wring
Some expiation for the thing
That he was yet to do. A chill
Struck helpless many a steadfast will
Within the ranks; the very air
Rang with a thunder-toned despair:
The hills seemed wandering to and fro,
Like lost guides blinded by the snow.

v

Yet faithful still 'mid woe and doubt
　One woman's loyal heart — whose pain
Filled it with pure celestial light —
Shone starry-constant like the North,
　Or that still radiance beaming forth
　From sacred lights in some lone fane.

But he whose ring Jemima wore,
By want and weariness all unstrung,
Though strong and honest of heart and young,
Shrank at the blast that pierced so frore —
Like a huge, invisible bird of prey
Furious launched from Labrador
And the granite cliffs of Saguenay!

Along the bleak Dead River's banks
They forced amain their frozen way;
But ever from the thinning ranks
Shapes of ice would reel and fall,
Human shapes, whose dying prayer
Floated, a mute white mist, in air;
The crowding snow their pall.

Spectre-like Famine drew near;
Her doom-word hummed in his ear:
Ah, weak were woman's hands to reach
And save him from the hellish charms
And wizard motion of those arms!
Yet only noble womanhood
The wife her dauntless part could teach:
She shared with him the last dry food
And thronged with hopefulness her speech,

As when hard by her home the flood
Of rushing Conestoga fills
Its depth afresh from springtide rills!

All, all in vain!
For far behind the invading rout
   These two were left alone;
And in the waste their wildest shout
   Seemed but a smothered groan.
Like sheeted wanderers from the grave
They moved, and yet seemed not to stir,
As icy gorge and sere-leaf'd grove
Of withered oak and shrouded fir
Were passed, and onward still they strove;
While the loud wind's artillery clave
The air, and furious sleety rain
Swung like a sword above the plain!

VI

They crossed the hills; they came to where
Through an arid gloom the river Chaudière
Fled like a Mænad with outstreaming hair;
And there the soldier sank, and died.

Death-dumb he fell; yet ere life sped,
Child-like on her knee he laid his head.
She strove to pray; but all words fled
Save those their love had sanctified.

And then her voice rose waveringly
To the notes of a mother's lullaby;
But her song was only "Ah, must thou
    die?"
And to her his eyes death-still replied.

VII

Dead leaves and stricken boughs
She heaped o'er the fallen form —
Wolf nor hawk nor lawless storm
Him from his rest should rouse;
But first, with solemn vows,
Took rifle, pouch, and horn,
And the belt that he had worn.
Then, onward pressing fast
Through the forest rude and vast,
Hunger-wasted, fever-parch'd,
Many bitter days she marched

With bleeding feet that spurned the flinty pain;
One thought always throbbing through her
    brain :
" They shall never say, ' He was afraid,' —
They shall never cry, ' The coward stayed ! ' "

VIII

Now the wilderness is passed;
Now the first hut reached, at last.

Ho, dwellers by the frontier trail,
Come forth and greet the bride of war !
From cabin and rough settlement
They come to speed her on her way —
Maidens, whose ruddy cheeks grow pale
With pity never felt before;
Children that cluster at the door;
Mothers, whose toil-worn hands are lent
To help, or bid her longer stay.
But through them all she passes on,
Strangely martial, fair and wan;
Nor waits to listen to their cheers
That sound so faintly in her ears.

For now all scenes around her shift,
Like those before a racer's eyes
When, foremost sped and madly swift,
Quick stretching toward the goal he flies,
Yet feels his strength wane with his
    breath,
And purpose fail 'mid fears of death,—

Till, like the flashing of a lamp,
Starts forth the sight of Arnold's camp,—
The bivouac flame, and sinuous gleam
Of steel,— where, crouched, the army waits,
Ere long, beyond the midnight stream,
To storm Quebec's ice-mounded gates.

IX

Then to the leader she was brought,
And spoke her simply loyal thought.
If, 'mid the shame of after-days,
The man who wronged his country's trust
(Yet now in worth outweighed all praise)
Remembered what this woman wrought,
It should have bowed him to the dust!

" Humbly my soldier-husband tried
To do his part.   He served,— and died.
But honor did not die.   His name
And honor — bringing both, I came;
And this his rifle, here, to show,
While far away the tired heart sleeps,
To-day his faith with you he keeps!"

Proudly the war-bride, ending so,
Sank breathless in the dumb white snow.

A RUNE OF THE RAIN

O many-tonèd rain!
O myriad sweet voices of the rain!
How welcome is its delicate overture
At evening, when the moist and glowing west
Seals all things with cool promise of night's rest.

At first it would allure
The earth to kinder mood,
With dainty flattering
Of soft, sweet pattering:
Faintly now you hear the tramp
Of the fine drops, falling damp
On the dry, sun-seasoned ground
And the thirsty leaves, resound.
But anon, imbued
With a sudden, bounding access
Of passion, it relaxes
All timider persuasion,
And, with nor pretext nor occasion,

Its wooing redoubles;
And pounds the ground, and bubbles
In sputtering spray,
Flinging itself in a fury
Of flashing white away;
Till the dusty road,
Dank-perfumed, is o'erflowed;
And the grass, and the wide-hung
    trees,
The vines, the flowers in their beds,—
The virid corn that to the breeze
Rustles along the garden-rows,—
Visibly lift their heads,
And, as the quick shower wilder grows,
Upleap with answering kisses to the rain.

Then, the slow and pleasant murmur
Of its subsiding,
As the pulse of the storm beats firmer,
And the steady rain
Drops into a cadenced chiding!
Deep-breathing rain,
The sad and ghostly noise
Wherewith thou dost complain —
Thy plaintive, spiritual voice,

Heard thus at close of day
Through vaults of twilight gray —
Vexes me with sweet pain;
And still my soul is fain
To know the secret of that yearning
Which in thine utterance I hear returning.
Hush, oh hush!
Break not the dreamy rush
Of the rain:
Touch not the marring doubt
Words bring to the certainty
Of its soft refrain;
But let the flying fringes flout
Their drops against the pane,
And the gurgling throat of the water-spout
Groan in the eaves amain.

The earth is wedded to the shower;
Darkness and awe gird round the bridal hour!

II

O many-tonèd rain!
It hath caught the strain

Of a wilder tune,
Ere the same night's noon,
When dreams and sleep forsake me,
And sudden dread doth wake me,
To hear the booming drums of heaven beat
The long roll to battle; when the knotted
    cloud,
With an echoing loud,
Bursts asunder
At the sudden resurrection of the thunder;
And the fountains of the air,
Unsealed again, sweep, ruining, everywhere,
To wrap the world in a watery winding-sheet.

III

O myriad sweet voices of the rain!
When the airy war doth wane,
And the storm to the east hath flown,
Cloaked close in the whirling wind,
There 's a voice still left behind
In each heavy-hearted tree,
Charged with tearful memory
Of the vanished rain:

From their leafy lashes wet
Drip the dews of fresh regret
For the lover that 's gone!
All else is still;
Yet the stars are listening,
And low o'er the wooded hill
Hangs, upon listless wing
Outspread, a shape of damp, blue cloud,
Watching, like a bird of evil
That knows nor mercy nor reprieval,
The slow and silent death of the pallid
    moon.

IV

But soon, returning duly,
Dawn whitens the wet hilltops bluely.
To her vision pure and cold
The night's wild tale is told
On the glistening leaf, in the mid-road pool,
The garden mold turned dark and cool,
And the meadows' trampled acres.
But hark, how fresh the song of the wingèd
    music-makers!

For now the moanings bitter,
Left by the rain, make harmony
With the swallow's matin-twitter,
And the robin's note, like the wind's in a tree.
The infant morning breathes sweet breath,
And with it is blent
The wistful, wild, moist scent
Of the grass in the marsh which the sea nourisheth:
And behold!
The last reluctant drop of the storm,
Wrung from the roof, is smitten warm
And turned to gold;
For in its veins doth run
The very blood of the bold, unsullied sun!

BREAKERS

Far out at sea there has been a storm,
And still, as they roll their liquid acres,
High-heaped the billows lower and glisten.
The air is laden, moist, and warm
With the dying tempest's breath;
And, as I walk the lonely strand
With sea-weed strewn, my forehead fanned
By wet salt-winds, I watch the breakers,
Furious sporting, tossed and tumbling,
Shatter here with a dreadful rumbling —
Watch, and muse, and vainly listen
To the inarticulate mumbling
Of the hoary-headed deep;
For who may tell me what it saith,
Muttering, moaning as in sleep?

Slowly and heavily
Comes in the sea,
With memories of storm o'erfreighted,
With heaving heart and breath abated,

Pregnant with some mysterious, endless sorrow,
And seamed with many a gaping, sighing furrow.

   Slowly and heavily
Grows the green water-mound;
But drawing ever nigher,
Towering ever higher,
Swollen with an inward rage
Naught but ruin can assuage,
Swift, now, without sound,
Creeps stealthily
Up to the shore—
Creeps, creeps and undulates;
As one dissimulates
Till, swayed by hateful frenzy,
Through passion grown immense, he
Bursts forth hostilely;
And rising, a smooth billow —
Its swelling, sunlit dome
Thinned to a tumid ledge
With keen, curved edge
Like the scornful curl
Of lips that snarl —
O'ertops itself and breaks
Into a raving foam;

So springs upon the shore
With a hungry roar;
Its first fierce anger slakes
On the stony shallow;
And runs up on the land,
Licking the smooth, hard sand,
Relentless, cold, yet wroth;
And dies in savage froth.

Then with its backward swirl
The sands and the stones, how they whirl!
O, fiercely doth it draw
Them to its chasm'd maw,
And against it in vain
They linger and strain;
And as they slip away
Into the seething gray
Fill all the thunderous air
With the horror of their despair,
And their wild terror wreak
In one hoarse, wailing shriek.

But scarce is this done,
When another one
Falls like the bolt from a bellowing gun,

And sucks away the shore
As that did before:
And another shall smother it o'er.

Then there 's a lull — a half-hush;
And forward the little waves rush,
Toppling and hurrying,
Each other worrying,
And in their haste
Run to waste.

Yet again is heard the trample
Of the surges high and ample:
Their dreadful meeting —
The wild and sudden breaking —
The dinting, and battering, and beating,
And swift forsaking.

And ever they burst and boom,
A numberless host;
Like heralds of doom
To the trembling coast;
And ever the tangled spray
Is tossed from the fierce affray,

And, as with spectral arms
That taunt and beckon and mock,
And scatter vague alarms,
Clasps and unclasps the rock;
Listlessly over it wanders;
Moodily, madly maunders,
And hissingly falls
From the glistening walls.

So all day along the shore
Shout the breakers, green and hoar,
Weaving out their weird tune;
Till at night the full moon
Weds the dark with that ring
Of gold that you see her fling
On the misty air.
Then homeward slow returning
To slumbers deep I fare,
Filled with an infinite yearning,
With thoughts that rise and fall
To the sound of the sea's hollow call,
Breathed now from white-lit waves that reach
Cold fingers o'er the damp, dark beach,
To scatter a spray on my dreams;

Till the slow and measured rote
Brings a drowsy ease
To my spirit, and seems
To set it soothingly afloat
On broad and buoyant seas
Of endless rest, lulled by the dirge
Of the melancholy surge.

BLACKMOUTH, OF COLORADO

" Who is Blackmouth ? " Well, that 's hard to say.
Mebbe he might ha' told you, 't other day,
If you 'd been here.   Now,— he 's gone away.
Come to think on, 't would n't ha' been no use
If you 'd called here earlier.   His excuse
Always was, whenever folks would ask him
Where he hailed from, an' *would* tease an' task
    him ; —
What d' you s'pose ?   He just said, " I don' know."

That was truth.   He came here long ago ;
But, before that, he 'd been born somewhere :
The conundrum started first, right there.
Little shaver — afore he knew his name
Or the place from whereabouts he came —
On a wagon-train the Apaches caught him.
Killed the old folks !   But this cus' — they brought
    him

Safe away from fire an' knife an' arrows.
So'thin' 'bout him must have touched their mar-
　　rows:
They was merciful; — treated him real good;
Brought him up to man's age well 's they
　　could.
Now, d' you b'lieve me, that there likely lad,
For all they used him so, went to the bad:
Leastways left the red men, that he knew,
'N' come to look for folks like me an' you; —
Goldarned white folks that he never saw.
Queerest thing was — though he loved a squaw,
'T was on her account he planned escape;
Shook the Apaches, an' took up red tape
With the U. S. gov'ment arter a while;
Tho' they do say gov'ment may be vile,
Mean an' treacherous an' deceivin'. Well,
I ain't sayin' our gov'ment is a sell.

Bocanegra — Spanish term — I 've heard
Stands for " Blackmouth." Now this curious bird,
Known as Bocanegra, gave his life
Most for others. First, he saved his wife;
Her I spoke of; — nothin' but a squaw.
You might wonder by what sort of law

He, a white man born, should come to love her.
But 't was somehow so: he *did* discover
Beauty in her, of the holding kind.
Some men love the light, an' some the shade.
Round that little Indian girl there played
Soft an' shadowy tremblings, like the dark
Under trees; yet now an' then a spark,
Quick 's a firefly, flashing from her eyes,   .
Made you think of summer-midnight skies.
She was faithful, too, like midnight stars.
As for Blackmouth, if you 'd seen the scars
Made by wounds he suffered for her sake,
You 'd have called *him* true, and no mistake.

    Growin' up a man, he scarcely met
Other white folks; an' his heart was set
On this red girl.   Yet he said: "We 'll wait.
You must never be my wedded mate
Till we reach the white man's country.   There,
Everything that 's done is fair and square."
Patiently they stayed, thro' trust or doubt,
Till tow'rds Colorado he could scout
Some safe track.   He told her: "You go first.
All my joy goes with you: — that 's the worst!
But *I* wait, to guard or hide the trail."

Indians caught him; an' they gave him — hail;
Cut an' tortured him, till he was bleeding;
Yet they found that still they were n't succeeding.
"Where 's that squaw?" they asked. "We 'll
        have her blood!
Either that, or grind you into mud;
Pick your eyes out, too, if you can't see
Where she 's gone to. Which, now, shall it be?
Tell us where she 's hid."

                "I 'll show the way,"
Blackmouth says; an' leads toward dawn of day,
Till they come straight out beside the brink
Of a precipice that seems to sink
Into everlasting gulfs below.
"Loose me!" Blackmouth tells 'em.   "But go
        slow."
Then they loosed him; and, with one swift leap,
Blackmouth swooped right down into the deep; —
Jumped out into space beyond the edge,
While the Apaches cowered along the ledge.
Seven hundred feet, they say. That 's guff!
Seventy foot, I tell you, 's 'bout enough.
Indians called him a dead antelope;
But they could n't touch the bramble-slope

Where he, bruised and stabbed, crawled under
    brush.
Their hand was beat hollow: *he* held a flush.

Day and night he limped or crawled along:
Winds blew hot, yet sang to him a song
(So he told me, once) that gave him hope.
Every time he saw a shadow grope
Down the hillsides, from a flying cloud,
Something touched his heart that made him proud:
Seemed to him he saw her dusky face
Watching over him, from place to place.
Every time the dry leaves rustled near,
Seemed to him she whispered, " Have no fear! "

So at last he found her: — they were married.
But, from those days on, he always carried
Marks of madness; actually — yes! —
Trusted the good faith of these U. S.

Indian hate an' deviltry he braved;
'N' scores an' scores of white men's lives he
    saved.
Just for that, his name should be engraved.
But it won't be! U. S. gov'ment dreads
Men who 're taller 'n politicians' heads.

All the while, his wife — tho' half despised
By the frontier folks that civilized
An' converted her — served by his side,
Helping faithfully, until she died.
Left alone, he lay awake o' nights,
Thinkin' what they 'd both done for the whites.
Then he thought of her, and Indian people;
Tryin' to measure, by the church's steeple,
Just how Christian our great nation 's been
Toward those native tribes so full of sin.
When he counted all the wrongs we 've done
To the wild men of the setting sun,
Seem'd to him the gov'ment wa'n't quite fair.
When its notes came due, it wa'n't right there.
U. S. gov'ment promised Indians lots,
But at last it closed accounts with shots.
Mouth was black, perhaps; — but *he* was white.
Calling gov'ment black don't seem polite:
Yet I 'll swear, its actions would n't show
'Longside Blackmouth's better 'n soot with snow.

Yes, sir! Blackmouth took the other side:
Honestly for years an' years he tried
Getting justice for the Indians. He,
Risking life an' limb for you an' me; —

He, the man who proved his good intent
By his deeds, an' plainly showed he meant
He would die for us,— turned round an' said:
" White men have been saved. Now, save the red!"
But it did n't pan out. No one would hark.
" Let the prairie-dogs an' Blackmouth bark,"
Said our folks. And — no, he wa'n't resigned,
But concluded he had missed his find.

"*Where* is Blackmouth ? " That I can't decide.
Red an' white men, both, he tried to serve;
But I guess, at last, he lost his nerve.
Kind o' tired out. See ? He had his pride :
Gave his life for others, far 's he could,
Hoping it would do 'em some small good.
Did n't seem to be much use. An' so —
Well; you see that man, dropped in the snow,
Where the crowd is ? Suicide, they say.
Looks as though he had quit work, to stay.
Bullet in the breast.— His *body* 's there;
But poor Blackmouth 's gone — I don't know
      where !

THE CHILD-YEAR

" Dying of hunger and sorrow :
   I die for my youth, I fear ! "
Murmured the midnight-haunting
   Voice of the stricken Year.

There like a child it perished
   In the stormy thoroughfare :
The snow with cruel whiteness
   Had aged its flowing hair.

Ah, little Year so fruitful,
   Ah, child that brought us bliss,
Must we so early lose you —
   Our dear hopes end in this ?

II

" Too young am I, too tender,
  To bear earth's avalanche
Of wrong, that grinds down life-hope,
  And makes my heart's-blood blanch.

" Tell him who soon shall follow
  Where my tired feet have bled,
He must be older, shrewder,
  Hard, cold, and selfish-bred —

" Or else like me be trampled
  Under the harsh world's heel.
'T is weakness to be youthful;
  'T is death to love and feel."

III

Then saw I how the New Year
  Came like a scheming man,
With icy eyes, his forehead
  Wrinkled by care and plan

For trade and rule and profit.
　To him the fading child
Looked up and cried, " Oh, brother!"
　But died even while it smiled.

Down bent the harsh new-comer
　To lift with loving arm
The wanderer mute and fallen;
　And lo! his eyes were warm;

All changed he grew; the wrinkles
　Vanished: he, too, looked young —
As if that lost child's spirit
　Into his breast had sprung.

So are those lives not wasted,
　Too frail to bear the fray.
So Years may die, yet leave us
　Young hearts in a world grown gray.

CHRISTENING

To-day I saw a little, calm-eyed child,—
  Where soft lights rippled and the shadows
      tarried
Within a church's shelter arched and aisled,—
  Peacefully wondering, to the altar carried;

White-robed and sweet, in semblance of a flower;
  White as the daisies that adorned the chancel;
Borne like a gift, the young wife's natural dower,
  Offered to God as her most precious hansel.

Then ceased the music, and the little one
  Was silent, with the multitude assembled
Hearkening; and when of Father and of Son
  He spoke, the pastor's deep voice broke and
      trembled.

But she, the child, knew not the solemn words,
  And suddenly yielded to a troublous wailing,
As helpless as the cry of frightened birds
  Whose untried wings for flight are unavailing.

How much the same, I thought, with older folk!
　The blessing falls: we call it tribulation,
And fancy that we wear a sorrow's yoke,
　Even at the moment of our consecration.

Pure daisy-child! Whatever be the form
　Of dream or doctrine,— or of unbelieving,—
A hand may touch our heads, amid the storm
　Of grief and doubt, to bless beyond bereaving;

A voice may sound, in measured, holy rite
　Of speech we know not, tho' its earnest meaning
Be clear as dew, and sure as starry light
　Gathered from some far-off celestial gleaning.

Wise is the ancient sacrament that blends
　This weakling cry of children in our churches
With strength of prayer or anthem that ascends
　　To Him who hearts of men and children
　　searches;

Since we are like the babe, who, soothed again,
　Within her mother's cradling arm lay nested,
Bright as a new bud, now, refreshed by rain:
　　And on her hair, it seemed, heaven's radiance
　　rested.

THANKSGIVING TURKEY

Valleys lay in sunny vapor,
   And a radiance mild was shed
From each tree that like a taper
   At a feast stood. Then we said,
" Our feast, too, shall soon be spread,
     Of good Thanksgiving turkey."

And already still November
   Drapes her snowy table here.
Fetch a log, then; coax the ember;
   Fill your hearts with old-time cheer;
   Heaven be thanked for one more year,
     And our Thanksgiving turkey!

Welcome, brothers—all our party
   Gathered in the homestead old!
Shake the snow off and with hearty
   Hand-shakes drive away the cold;
   Else your plate you'll hardly hold
     Of good Thanksgiving turkey.

When the skies are sad and murky,
  'T is a cheerful thing to meet
Round this homely roast of turkey—
  Pilgrims, pausing just to greet,
  Then, with earnest grace, to eat
    A new Thanksgiving turkey.

And the merry feast is freighted
  With its meanings true and deep.
Those we 've loved and those we 've hated,
  All, to-day, the rite will keep,
  All, to-day, their dishes heap
    With plump Thanksgiving turkey.

But how many hearts must tingle
  Now with mournful memories!
In the festal wine shall mingle
  Unseen tears, perhaps from eyes
  That look beyond the board where lies
    Our plain Thanksgiving turkey.

See around us, drawing nearer,
  Those faint yearning shapes of air—
Friends than whom earth holds none dearer!
  No—alas! they are not there:

Have they, then, forgot to share
Our good Thanksgiving turkey?

Some have gone away and tarried
Strangely long by some strange wave;
Some have turned to foes; we carried
Some unto the pine-girt grave:
They 'll come no more so joyous-brave
To take Thanksgiving turkey.

Nay, repine not. Let our laughter
Leap like firelight up again.
Soon we touch the wide Hereafter,
Snow-field yet untrod of men:
Shall we meet once more—and when?—
To eat Thanksgiving turkey.

BEFORE THE SNOW

Autumn is gone: through the blue woodlands
    bare
  Shatters the rainy wind. A myriad leaves,
Like birds that fly the mournful Northern air,
  Flutter away from the old forest's eaves.

Autumn is gone: as yonder silent rill,
  Slow eddying o'er thick leaf-heaps lately shed,
My spirit, as I walk, moves awed and still,
  By thronging fancies wild and wistful led.

Autumn is gone: alas, how long ago
  The grapes were plucked, and garnered was
    the grain!
How soon death settles on us, and the snow
  Wraps with its white alike our graves, our
    gain!

84

Yea, autumn's gone!   Yet it robs not my mood
  Of that which makes moods dear,—some shoot
      of spring
Still sweet within me; or thoughts of yonder
      wood
  We walked in,—memory's rare environing.

And, though they die, the seasons only take
  A ruined substance.   All that's best remains
In the essential vision that can make
  One light for life, love, death, their joys, their
      pains.

III

YOUTH TO THE POET

(TO OLIVER WENDELL HOLMES)

Strange spell of youth for age, and age for youth,
Affinity between two forms of truth !—
As if the dawn and sunset watched each other,
Like and unlike as children of one mother
And wondering at the likeness. Ardent eyes
Of young men see the prophecy arise
Of what their lives shall be when all is told;
And, in the far-off glow of years called old,
Those other eyes look back to catch a trace
Of what was once their own unshadowed grace.
But here in our dear poet both are blended—
Ripe age begun, yet golden youth not ended;—
Even as his song the willowy scent of spring
Doth blend with autumn's tender mellowing,
And mixes praise with satire, tears with fun,
In strains that ever delicately run;
So musical and wise, page after page,
The sage a minstrel grows, the bard a sage.

The dew of youth fills yet his late-sprung flowers,
And day-break glory haunts his evening hours.
Ah, such a life prefigures its own moral:
That first " Last Leaf" is now a leaf of laurel,
Which — smiling not, but trembling at the touch —
Youth gives back to the hand that gave so much.

EVENING OF DECEMBER 3, 1879.

THE SWORD DHAM

"How shall we honor the man who creates?"
 Asked the Bedouin chief, the poet Antar; —
"Who unto the truth flings open our gates,
  Or fashions new thoughts from the light of a
   star;
 Or forges with craft of his finger and brain
 Some marvelous weapon we copy in vain;
 Or chants to the winds a wild song that shall
  wander forever undying?

"See! His reward is in envies and hates;
 In lips that deny, or in stabs that may kill."
"Nay," said the smith; "for there's one here who
  waits
  Humbly to serve you with unmeasured skill,
 Sure that no utmost devotion can fail,
 Offered to *you*, nor unfriended assail
 The heart of the hero and poet Antar, whose
  fame is undying!"

" Speak," said the chief.   Then the smith: "O
    Antar,
    It is I who would serve you! I know, by
    the soul
Of the poet within you, no envy can bar
    The stream of your gratitude,—once let it
    roll.
Listen.   The lightning, your camel that slew,
    I caught, and wrought in this sword-blade for
    you;—
Sword that no foe shall encounter unhurt, or
    depart from undying."

Burst from the eyes of Antar a swift rain,—
    Gratitude's glittering drops,— as he threw
One shining arm round the smith, like a chain.
    Closer the man to his bosom he drew;
Thankful, caressing, with " Great is my debt."
    " Yea," said the smith, and his eyelids were
    wet:
" I knew the sword Dham would unite me with
    you in an honor undying."

" So ? " asked the chief, as his thumb-point at will
    Silently over the sword's edge played.

—" Ay!" said the smith, " but there 's one thing,
   still :
Who is the smiter, shall smite with this blade?"
Jealous, their eyes met; and fury awoke.
" *I* am the smiter!" Antar cried.   One stroke
Rolled the smith's head from his neck, and gave
   him remembrance undying.

" Seek now who may, no search will avail :
   No man the mate of this weapon shall own!"
Yet, in his triumph, the chieftain made wail :
   "Slain is the craftsman, the one friend alone
Able to honor the man who creates.
   I slew him — *I*, who am poet!   O fates,
Grant that the envious blade slaying artists shall
   make them undying!"

"AT THE GOLDEN GATE"

Before the golden gate she stands,
With drooping head, with idle hands
Loose-clasped, and bent beneath the weight
Of unseen woe. Too late, too late!
    Those carved and fretted,
    Starred, rosetted
Panels shall not open ever
To her who seeks the perfect mate.

Only the tearless enter there:
Only the soul that, like a prayer,
No bolt can stay, no wall may bar,
Shall dream the dreams grief cannot mar.
    No door of cedar,
    Alas, shall lead her
Unto the stream that shows forever
Love's face like some reflected star!

They say that golden barrier hides
A realm where deathless spring abides;

Where flowers shall fade not, and there floats
Thro' moon-rays mild or sunlit motes—
    'Mid dewy alleys
    That gird the palace,
And fountain'd spray's unceasing quiver—
A dulcet rain of song-birds' notes.

The sultan lord knew not her name;
But to the door that fair shape came:
The hour had struck, the way was right,
Traced by her lamp's pale, flickering light.
    But ah, whose error
    Has brought this terror?
Whose fault has foiled her fond endeavor?
The gate swings to: her hope takes flight.

The harp, the song, the nightingales
She hears, beyond. The night-wind wails
Without, to sound of feast within,
While here she stands, shut out by sin.
    And be that revel
    Of angel or devil,
She longs to sit beside the giver,
That she at last her prize may win.

Her lamp has fallen; her eyes are wet;
Frozen she stands, she lingers yet;
But through the garden's gladness steals
A whisper that each heart congeals —
  A moan of grieving
  Beyond relieving,
Which makes the proudest of them shiver.
And suddenly the sultan kneels!

The lamp was quenched; he found her dead,
When dawn had turned the threshold red.
 Her face was calm and sad as fate:
 His sin, not hers, made her too late.
  Some think, unbidden
  She brought him, hidden,
 A truer bliss that came back never
 To him, unblest, who closed the gate.

CHARITY

I

Unarmed she goeth ; yet her hands
Strike deeper awe than steel-caparison'd bands.
   No fatal hurt of foe she fears,—
Veiled, as with mail, in mist of gentle tears.

II

'Gainst her thou canst not bar the door :
Like air she enters, where none dared before.
   Even to the rich she can forgive
Their regal selfishness,— and let them live !

HELEN AT THE LOOM

Helen, in her silent room,
Weaves upon the upright loom;
Weaves a mantle rich and dark,
Purpled over, deep. But mark
How she scatters o'er the wool
Woven shapes, till it is full
Of men that struggle close, complex;
Short-clipp'd steeds with wrinkled necks
Arching high; spear, shield, and all
The panoply that doth recall
Mighty war; such war as e'en
For Helen's sake is waged, I ween.
Purple is the groundwork: good!
All the field is stained with blood —
Blood poured out for Helen's sake;
(Thread, run on; and shuttle, shake!)
But the shapes of men that pass
Are as ghosts within a glass,
Woven with whiteness of the swan,
Pale, sad memories, gleaming wan

From the garment's purple fold
Where Troy's tale is twined and told.
Well may Helen, as with tender
Touch of rosy fingers slender
She doth knit the story in
Of Troy's sorrow and her sin,
Feel sharp filaments of pain
Reeled off with the well-spun skein,
And faint blood-stains on her hands
From the shifting, sanguine strands.

Gently, sweetly she doth sorrow:
What has been must be to-morrow;
Meekly to her fate she bows.
Heavenly beauties still will rouse
Strife and savagery in men:
Shall the lucid heavens, then,
Lose their high serenity,
Sorrowing over what must be?
If she taketh to her shame,
Lo, they give her not the blame,—
Priam's wisest counselors,
Aged men, not loving wars.
When she goes forth, clad in white,
Day-cloud touched by first moonlight,

With her fair hair, amber-hued
As vapor by the moon imbued
With burning brown, that round her clings,
See, she sudden silence brings
On the gloomy whisperers
Who would make the wrong all hers.
So, Helen, in thy silent room,
Labor at the storied loom;
(Thread, run on; and shuttle, shake!)
Let thy aching sorrow make
Something strangely beautiful
Of this fabric; since the wool
Comes so tinted from the Fates,
Dyed with loves, hopes, fears, and hates.
Thou shalt work with subtle force
All thy deep shade of remorse
In the texture of the weft,
That no stain on thee be left; —
Ay, false queen, shalt fashion grief,
Grief and wrong, to soft relief.
Speed the garment! It may chance,
Long hereafter, meet the glance,
Of Œnone; when her lord,
Now thy Paris, shall go tow'rd
Ida, at his last sad end,
Seeking her, his early friend,

Who alone can cure his ill,
Of all who love him, if she will.
It were fitting she should see
In that hour thine artistry,
And her husband's speechless corse
In the garment of remorse!

But take heed that in thy work
Naught unbeautiful may lurk.
Ah, how little signifies
Unto thee what fortunes rise,
What others fall! Thou still shalt rule,
Still shalt twirl the colored spool.
Though thy yearning woman's eyes
Burn with glorious agonies,
Pitying the waste and woe,
And the heroes falling low
In the war around thee, here,
Yet the least, quick-trembling tear
'Twixt thy lids shall dearer be
Than life, to friend or enemy.

There are people on the earth
Doomed with doom of too great worth.
Look on Helen not with hate,
Therefore, but compassionate.

If she suffer not too much,
Seldom does she feel the touch
Of that fresh, auroral joy
Lighter spirits may decoy
To their pure and sunny lives.
Heavy honey 't is she hives.
To her sweet but burdened soul
All that here she may control—
What of bitter memories,
What of coming fate's surmise,
Paris' passion, distant din
Of the war now drifting in
To her quiet—idle seems;
Idle as the lazy gleams
Of some stilly water's reach,
Seen from where broad vine-leaves pleach
A heavy arch; and, looking through,
Far away the doubtful blue
Glimmers, on a drowsy day,
Crowded with the sun's rich gray;—
As she stands within her room,
Weaving, weaving at the loom.

THE CASKET OF OPALS

Deep, smoldering colors of the land and sea
Burn in these stones, that, by some mystery,
Wrap fire in sleep and never are consumed.
Scarlet of daybreak, sunset gleams half spent
In thick white cloud; pale moons that may have
    lent
Light to love's grieving; rose-illumined snows,
And veins of gold no mine depth ever gloomed;
All these, and green of thin-edged waves, are there.
I think a tide of feeling through them flows
With blush and pallor, as if some being of air,—
Some soul once human,— wandering, in the snare
Of passion had been caught, and henceforth
    doomed
In misty crystal here to lie entombed.

And so it is, indeed. Here prisoned sleep
The ardors and the moods and all the pain
That once within a man's heart throbbed. He
    gave

These opals to the woman whom he loved;
And now, like glinting sunbeams through the rain,
The rays of thought that through his spirit moved
Leap out from these mysterious forms again.

The colors of the jewels laugh and weep
As with his very voice. In them the wave
Of sorrow and joy that, with a changing sweep,
Bore him to misery or else made him blest
Still surges in melodious, wild unrest.
So when each gem in place I touch and take,
It murmurs what he thought or what he spake.

FIRST OPAL

My heart is like an opal
Made to lie upon your breast
In dreams of ardor, clouded o'er
By endless joy's unrest.

And forever it shall haunt you
With its mystic, changing ray:
Its light shall live when we lie dead,
With hearts at the heart of day!

SECOND OPAL

If, from a careless hold,
  One gem of these should fall,
No power of art or gold
  Its wholeness could recall:
The lustrous wonder dies
  In gleams of irised rain,
As light fades out from the eyes
  When a soul is crushed by pain.
Take heed that from your hold
  My love you do not cast:
Dim, shattered, vapor-cold —
  That day would be its last.

II

THIRD OPAL

He won her love ; and so this opal sings
With all its tints in maze, that seem to quake
And leap in light, as if its heart would break :

Gleam of the sea,
Translucent air,
Where every leaf alive with glee

Glows in the sun without shadow of grief—
You speak of spring,
When earth takes wing
And sunlight, sunlight is everywhere!
Radiant life,
Face so fair —
Crowned with the gracious glory of wife—
Your glance lights all this happy day,
Your tender glow
And murmurs low
Make miracle, miracle, everywhere.

Earth takes wing
With birds—do I care
Whether of sorrow or joy they sing?
No; for they make not my life nor destroy!
My soul awakes
At a smile that breaks
In sun; and sunlight is everywhere!

III

Then dawned a mood of musing thoughtful-
     ness ;
As if he doubted whether he could bless

Her wayward spirit, through each fickle hour,
With love's serenity of flawless power,
Or she remain a vision, as when first
She came to soothe his fancy all athirst.

FOURTH OPAL

We were alone : the perfumed night,
   Moonlighted, like a flower
Grew round us and exhaled delight
   To bless that one sweet hour.

You stood where, 'mid the white and gold,
   The rose-fire through the gloom
Touched hair and cheek and garment's fold
   With soft, ethereal bloom.

And when the vision seemed to swerve,
   'T was but the flickering shine
That gave new grace, a lovelier curve,
   To every dream-like line.

O perfect vision ! Form and face
   Of womanhood complete !

O rare ideal to embrace
And hold, from head to feet!

Could I so hold you ever — could
Your eye still catch the glow
Of mine — it were an endless good:
Together we should grow

One perfect picture of our love! . . .
Alas, the embers old
Fell, and the moonlight fell, above —
Dim, shattered, vapor-cold.

IV

What ill befell these lovers ?   Shall I say ?
What tragedy of petty care and sorrow ?
Ye all know, who have lived and loved : if nay,
Then those will know who live and love to-
morrow.
But here at least is what this opal said,
The fifth in number : and the next two bore
My fancy toward that dim world of the dead,
Where waiting spirits muse the past life
o'er :

FIFTH OPAL

I dreamed my kisses on your hair
Turned into roses. Circling bloom
Crowned the loose-lifted tresses there.
" O Love," I cried, " forever
Dwell wreathed, and perfume-haunted
By my heart's deep honey-breath ! "
But even as I bending looked, I saw
The roses were not; and, instead, there lay
Pale, feathered flakes and scentless
Ashes upon your hair !

SIXTH OPAL

The love I gave, the love I gave,
  Wherewith I sought to win you —
Ah, long and close to you it clave
  With life and soul and sinew !

My gentleness with scorn you cursed:
  You knew not what I gave.
The strongest man may die of thirst:
  My love is in its grave !

SEVENTH OPAL

You say these jewels were accurst —
  With evil omen fraught.
You should have known it from the first!
  This was the truth they taught:

No treasured thing in heaven or earth
  Holds potency more weird
Than our hearts hold, that throb from birth
  With wavering flames insphered.

And when from me the gems you took,
  On that strange April day,
My nature, too, I gave, that shook
  With passion's fateful play.

The mingled fate my love should give
  In these mute emblems shone,
That more intensely burn and live —
  While I am turned to stone.

v

Listen now to what is said
By the eighth opal, flashing red

And pale, by turns, with every breath —
The voice of the lover after death.

EIGHTH OPAL

I did not know before
    That we dead could rise and walk;
That our voices, as of yore,
    Would blend in gentle talk.

I did not know her eyes
    Would so haunt mine after death,
Or that she could hear my sighs,
    Low as the harp-string's breath.

But, ah, last night we met!
    From our stilly trance we rose,
Thrilled with all the old regret—
    The grieving that God knows.

She asked: "Am I forgiven?"—
    "And dost thou forgive?" I said,
Ah! how long for joy we 'd striven!
    But now our hearts were dead.

Alas, for the lips I kissed
And the sweet hope, long ago!
On her grave chill hangs the mist;
On mine, white lies the snow.

VI

Hearkening still, I hear this strain
From the ninth opal's varied vein:

NINTH OPAL

In the mountains of Mexico,
Where the barren volcanoes throw
Their fierce peaks high to the sky,
With the strength of a tawny brute
That sees heaven but to defy,
And the soft, white hand of the snow
Touches and makes them mute,—

Firm in the clasp of the ground
The opal is found.
By the struggle of frost and fire
Created, yet caught in a spell

From which only human desire
Can free it, what passion profound
In its dim, sweet bosom may dwell!

So was it with us, I think,
Whose souls were formed on the brink
Of a crater, where rain and flame
Had mingled and crystallized.
One venturous day Love came;
Found us; and bound with a link
Of gold the jewels he prized.

The agonies old of the earth,
Its plenitude and its dearth,
The torrents of flame and of tears,
All these in our souls were inborn.
And we must endure through the years
The glory and burden of birth
That filled us with fire of the morn.

Let the diamond lie in its mine;
Let ruby and topaz shine;
The beryl sleep, and the emerald keep
Its sunned-leaf green! We know
The joy of sufferings deep

That blend with a love divine,
And the hidden warmth of the snow!

TENTH OPAL

Colors that tremble and perish,
　Atoms that follow the law,
You mirror the truth which we cherish,
　You mirror the spirit we saw.
Glow of the daybreak tender,
　Flushed with an opaline gleam,
And passionate sunset-splendor—
　Ye both but embody a dream.
Visions of cloud-hidden glory
　Breaking from sources of light
Mimic the mist of life's story,
　Mingled of scarlet and white.
Sunset-clouds iridescent,
　Opals, and mists of the day,
Are thrilled alike with the crescent
　Delight of a deathless ray
Shot through the hesitant trouble
　Of particles floating in space,
And touching each wandering bubble
　With tints of a rainbowed grace.

So through the veil of emotion
  Trembles the light of the truth ;
And so may the light of devotion
  Glorify life — age and youth.
Sufferings, — pangs that seem cruel, —
  These are but atoms adrift :
The light streams through, and a jewel
  Is formed for us, Heaven's own gift !

LOVE THAT LIVES

Dear face — bright, glinting hair;
    Dear life, whose heart is mine —
The thought of you is prayer,
    The love of you divine.

In starlight, or in rain;
    In the sunset's shrouded glow;
Ever, with joy or pain,
    To you my quick thoughts go

Like winds or clouds, that fleet
    Across the hungry space
Between, and find you, sweet,
    Where life again wins grace.

Now, as in that once young
    Year that so softly drew
My heart to where it clung,
    I long for, gladden in you.

And when in the silent hours
  I whisper your sacred name,
Like an altar-fire it showers
  My blood with fragrant flame!

Perished is all that grieves;
  And lo, our old-new joys
Are gathered as in sheaves,
  Held in love's equipoise.

Ours is the love that lives;
  Its springtime blossoms blow
'Mid the fruit that autumn gives,
  And its life outlasts the snow.

IV

BLUEBIRD'S GREETING

Over the mossy walls,
Above the slumbering fields
Where yet the ground no fruitage yields,
Save as the sunlight falls
In dreams of harvest-yellow,
What voice remembered calls,—
So bubbling fresh, so soft and mellow?

A darting, azure-feathered arrow
From some lithe sapling's bow-curve, fleet
The bluebird, springing light and narrow,
Sings in flight, with gurglings sweet:

" Out of the South I wing,
Blown on the breath of Spring:
The little faltering song
That in my beak I bring
Some maiden shall catch and sing,
Filling it with the longing
And the blithe, unfettered thronging
Of her spirit's blossoming.

" Warbling along
In the sunny weather,
Float, my notes,
Through the sunny motes,
Falling light as a feather!
Flit, flit, o'er the fertile land
'Mid hovering insects' hums;
Fall into the sower's hand:
Then, when his harvest comes,
The seed and the song shall have flowered
    together.

" From the Coosa and Altamaha,
With a thought of the dim blue Gulf;
From the Roanoke and Kanawha;
From the musical Southern rivers,
O'er the land where the fierce war-wolf
Lies slain and buried in flowers;
I come to your chill, sad hours
And the woods where the sunlight shivers.
I come like an echo: 'Awake!'
I answer the sky and the lake
And the clear, cool color that quivers
In all your azure rills.
I come to your wan, bleak hills

For a greeting that rises dearer,
To homely hearts draws me nearer
Than the warmth of the rice-fields or wealth
  of the ranches.

" I will charm away your sorrow,
  For I sing of the dewy morrow :
  My melody sways like the branches
  My light feet set astir :
  I bring to the old, as I hover,
  The days and the joys that were,
  And hope to the waiting lover !
  Then, take my note and sing,
  Filling it with the longing
  And the blithe, unfettered thronging
  Of your spirit's blossoming ! "

Not long that music lingers :
Like the breath of forgotten singers
It flies,— or like the March-cloud's shadow
That sweeps with its wing the faded meadow
Not long ! And yet thy fleeting,
Thy tender, flute-toned greeting,
O bluebird, wakes an answer that remains
The purest chord in' all the year's refrains.

THE VOICE OF THE VOID

I warn, like the one drop of rain
On your face, ere the storm;
Or tremble in whispered refrain
  With your blood, beating warm.
I am the presence that ever
Baffles your touch's endeavor,—
Gone like the glimmer of dust
  Dispersed by a gust.
I am the absence that taunts you,
The fancy that haunts you;
The ever unsatisfied guess
That, questioning emptiness,
Wins a sigh for reply.
  Nay; nothing am I,
  But the flight of a breath —
    For I am Death!

"O WHOLESOME DEATH"

O wholesome Death, thy sombre funeral-car
  Looms ever dimly on the lengthening way
  Of life ; while, lengthening still, in sad array,
My deeds in long procession go, that are
As mourners of the man they helped to mar.
  I see it all in dreams, such as waylay
  The wandering fancy when the solid day
Has fallen in smoldering ruins, and night's star,
Aloft there, with its steady point of light
  Mastering the eye, has wrapped the brain in
      sleep.
Ah, when I die, and planets hold their flight
  Above my grave, still let my spirit keep
Sometimes its vigil of divine remorse,
' Midst pity, praise, or blame heaped o 'er my
    corse !

INCANTATION

When the leaves, by thousands thinned,
A thousand times have whirled in the wind,
And the moon, with hollow cheek,
Staring from her hollow height,
Consolation seems to seek
From the dim, reëchoing night;
And the fog-streaks dead and white
Lie like ghosts of lost delight
O'er highest earth and lowest sky;
Then, Autumn, work thy witchery!

Strew the ground with poppy-seeds,
And let my bed be hung with weeds,
Growing gaunt and rank and tall,
Drooping o'er me like a pall.
Send thy stealthy, white-eyed mist
Across my brow to turn and twist

Fold on fold, and leave me blind
To all save visions in the mind.
Then, in the depth of rain-fed streams
I shall slumber, and in dreams
Slide through some long glen that burns
With a crust of blood-red ferns
And brown-withered wings of brake
Like a burning lava-lake; —
So, urged to fearful, faster flow
By the awful gasp, "Hahk! hahk!" of the
    crow,
Shall pass by many a haunted rood
Of the nutty, odorous wood;
Or, where the hemlocks lean and loom,
Shall fill my heart with bitter gloom;
Till, lured by light, reflected cloud,
I burst aloft my watery shroud,
And upward through the ether sail
Far above the shrill wind's wail; —
But, falling thence, my soul involve
With the dust dead flowers dissolve;
And, gliding out at last to sea,
Lulled to a long tranquillity,
The perfect poise of seasons keep
With the tides that rest at neap.

So must be fulfilled the rite
That giveth me the dead year's might;
And at dawn I shall arise
A spirit, though with human eyes,
A human form and human face;
And where'er I go or stay,
There the summer's perished grace
Shall be with me, night and day.

FAMINE AND HARVEST

[PLYMOUTH PLANTATION: 1622]

The strong and the tender,
  The young and the old,
Unto Death we must render:—
  Our silver, our gold.

To break their long sleeping
  No voice may avail:
They hear not our weeping—
  Our famished love's wail.

Yea, those whom we cherish
  Depart, day by day.
Soon we, too, shall perish
  And crumble to clay.

And the vine and the berry
  Above us will bloom;

The wind shall make merry
 While we lie in gloom.

Fear not! Though thou starvest,
 Provision is made:
God gathers His harvest
 When our hopes fade!

THE CHILD'S WISH GRANTED

Do you remember, my sweet, absent son,
How in the soft June days forever done
You loved the heavens so warm and clear and
    high;
And when I lifted you, soft came your cry,—
" Put me 'way up — 'way, 'way up in blue sky"?

I laughed and said I could not;—set you down,
Your gray eyes wonder-filled beneath that crown
Of bright hair gladdening me as you raced by.
Another Father now, more strong than I,
Has borne you voiceless to your dear blue sky.

THE FLOWN SOUL

(FRANCIS HAWTHORNE LATHROP)

FEBRUARY 6, 1881

Come not again! I dwell with you
Above the realm of frost and dew,
Of pain and fire, and growth to death.
I dwell with you where never breath
Is drawn, but fragrance vital flows
From life to life, even as a rose
Unseen pours sweetness through each vein
And from the air distills again.
You are my rose unseen; we live
Where each to other joy may give
In ways untold, by means unknown
And secret as the magnet-stone.

For which of us, indeed, is dead?
No more I lean to kiss your head —
The gold-red hair so thick upon it;
Joy feels no more the touch that won it

When o'er my brow your pearl-cool palm
In tenderness so childish, calm,
Crept softly, once. Yet, see, my arm
Is strong, and still my blood runs warm.
I still can work, and think and weep.
But all this show of life I keep
Is but the shadow of your shine,
Flicker of your fire, husk of your vine;
Therefore, you are not dead, nor I
Who hear your laughter's minstrelsy.
Among the stars your feet are set;
Your little feet are dancing yet
Their rhythmic beat, as when on earth.
So swift, so slight are death and birth!

Come not again, dear child. If thou
By any chance couldst break that vow
Of silence at thy last hour made;
If to this grim life unafraid
Thou couldst return, and melt the frost
Wherein thy bright limbs' power was lost;
Still would I whisper — since so fair
This silent comradeship we share —
Yes, whisper 'mid the unbidden rain
Of tears: " Come not, come not again!"

SUNSET AND SHORE

Birds that like vanishing visions go winging,
  White, white in the flame of the sunset's burning,
Fly with the wild spray the billows are flinging,
  Blend, blend with the nightfall, and fade, un-
    returning!

Fire of the heaven, whose splendor all-glowing
  Soon, soon shall end, and in darkness must perish;
Sea-bird and flame-wreath and foam lightly blow-
    ing;—
  Soon, soon tho' we lose you, your beauty we
    cherish.

Visions may vanish, the sweetest, the dearest;
  Hush'd, hush'd be the voice of love's echo re-
    plying;
Spirits may leave us that clung to us nearest:—
  Love, love, only love dwells with us undying!

THE PHŒBE-BIRD

(A REPLY)

Yes, I was wrong about the phœbe-bird.
Two songs it has, and both of them I 've heard:
I did not know those strains of joy and sorrow
Came from one throat, or that each, note could
    borrow
Strength from the other, making one more brave
And one as sad as rain-drops on a grave.

But thus it is. Two songs have men and maidens:
One is for hey-day, one is sorrow's cadence.
Our voices vary with the changing seasons
Of life's long year, for deep and natural reasons.
Therefore despair not. Think not you have al-
    tered,
If, at some time, the gayer note has faltered.
We are as God has made us. Gladness, pain,
Delight and death, and moods of bliss or bane,

With love and hate, or good and evil—all,
At separate times, in separate accents call;
Yet 't is the same heart-throb within the breast
That gives an impulse to our worst and best.
I doubt not when our earthly cries are ended,
The Listener finds them in one music blended.

A STRONG CITY

For them that hope in Thee. . . . Thou shalt hide them in the secret of Thy face, from the disturbance of men.

Thou shalt protect them in Thy tabernacle from the contradiction of tongues.

Blessed be the Lord, for He hath shewn His wonderful mercy to me in a fortified city.   — *Psalm xxx.*

Beauty and splendor were on every hand:
Yet strangely crawled dark shadows down the
    lanes,
Twisting across the fields, like dragon-shapes
That smote the air with blackness, and devoured
The life of light, and choked the smiling world
Till it grew livid with a sudden age —
The death of hope.

           O squandered happiness;
Vain dust of misery powdering life's fresh flower!
The sky was holy, but the earth was not.

Men ruled, but ruled in vain; since wretchedness
Of soul and body, for the mass of men,

Made them like dead leaves in an idle drift
Around the plough of progress as it drove
Sharp through the glebe of modern days, to plant
A civilized world. Ay ; civilized — but not Christian!

   Civilization is a clarion voice
Crying in the wilderness ; a prophet-word
Still unfulfilled. And lo, along the ways
Crowded with nations, there arose a strife ;
Disturbance of men ; tongues contradicting tongues ;
Madness of noise, that scattered multitudes ;
A trample of blind feet, beneath whose tread
Truth's bloom shrank withered ; while incessant
    mouths
Howled " Progress ! Change ! "— as though all
    moods of change
Were fiats of truth eternal.

                  'Mid the din
Two pilgrims, faring forward, saw the light
In a strong city, fortified, and moved
Patiently thither. " All your steps are vain,"
Cried scoffers. " There is mercy in the world ;
But chiefly mercy of man to man. For we
Are good. We help our fellows, when we can.

Our charity is enormous. Look at these
Long rolls of rich subscriptions. We are good.
'T is true, God's mercy plays a part in things;
But most is left to us; and we judge well.
Stay with us in the field of endless war!
Here only is health. Yon city fortified
You dream of—why, its ramparts are as dust.
It gives no safety. One assaulting sweep
Of our huge cohorts would annul its power—
Crush it in atoms; make it meaningless."

  The pilgrims listened; but onward still they
      moved.
They passed the gates; they stood upon a hill
Enclosed, but in that strong enclosure free!
Though earth opposed, they held the key to heaven.
On came the turbulent multitude in war,
Dashing against the city's walls; and swept
Through all the streets, and robbed and burned
      and killed.
The walls were strong; the gates were always open.
And so the invader rioted, and was proud.
But sudden, in seeming triumph, the enemy host
Was stricken with death; and still the city stayed.
Skyward the souls of its defenders rose,

Returning soon in mist intangible
That flashed with radiance of half-hidden swords;
And those who still assaulted—though they crept
Into the inmost vantage-points, with craft—
Fell, blasted namelessly by this veiled flash,
Even as they shouted out, "The place is ours!"

So those two pilgrims dwelt there, fortified
In that strong city men had thought so frail.
They died, and lived again. Fiercest attack
Was as a perfumed breeze to them, which drew
Their souls still closer unto God. And there
Beauty and splendor bloomed untouched. The
    stars
Spoke to them, bidding them be of good cheer,
Though hostile hordes rushed over them in blood.
And still the prayers of all that people rose
As incense mingled with music of their hearts.
For Christ was with them: angels were their aid.
What though the enemy used their open gates?
The children of the citadel conquered all
Their conquerors, smiting them with the pure light
That shone in that strong city fortified.

THREE DOVES

Seaward, at morn, my doves flew free;
At eve they circled back to me.
The first was Faith; the second, Hope;
The third — the whitest — Charity.

Above the plunging surge's play
Dream-like they hovered, day by day.
At last they turned, and bore to me
Green signs of peace thro' nightfall gray.

No shore forlorn, no loveliest land
Their gentle eyes had left unscanned,
'Mid hues of twilight-heliotrope
Or daybreak fires by heaven-breath fanned.

Quick visions of celestial grace,—
Hither they waft, from earth's broad space,
Kind thoughts for all humanity.
They shine with radiance from God's face.

Ah, since my heart they choose for home,
Why loose them,—forth again to roam?
Yet look: they rise! with loftier scope
They wheel in flight toward heaven's pure dome.

Fly, messengers that find no rest
Save in such toil as makes man blest!
Your home is God's immensity:
We hold you but at his behest.

V

ARISE, AMERICAN!

The soul of a nation awaking,—
　　High visions of daybreak,—I saw;
　　　A people renewed; the forsaking
　　　　Of sin, and the worship of law.

Sing, pine-tree; shout, to the hoarser
　　Response of the jubilant sea!
　　　Rush, river, foam-flecked like a courser;
　　　　Warn all who are honest and free!

Our birth-star beckons to trial
　　The faith of the far-fled years,
　　　Ere scorn was our share, and denial,
　　　　Or laughter for patriots' tears.

And Faith shall come forth the finer,
　　From trampled thickets of fire,
　　　And the orient open diviner
　　　　Before her, the heaven rise higher.

O deep, sweet eyes, but severer
  Than steel! See you yet, where he comes —
    Our hero? Bend your glance nearer;
      Speak, Faith! For, as wakening drums,

Your voice shall set his blood stirring;
  His heart shall grow strong like the main
    When the rowelled winds are spurring,
      And the broad tides landward strain.

O hero, art thou among us?
  O helper, hidest thou, still?
    Why hast thou no anthem sung us,
      Why workest thou not our will?

For a smirk of the face, or a favor,
  Still shelters the cheat where he crawls;
    And the truth we began with needs braver
      Upholders, and loftier walls.

Too long has the land's soul slumbered
  In wearying dreams of gain,
    With prosperous falsity cumbered
      And dulled with bribes, as a bane.

Yes, cunning is civilized evil,
  And crafty the gold-baited snare;
    But virtue, in fiery upheaval,
      May cast fine device to the air.

Bring us the simple and stalwart
  Purpose of earlier days.
    Come! Far better than all were 't —
      Our precepts, our pride, and our lays —

That the people in spirit should tremble
  With heed of the God-given Word;
    That we cease from our boast, nor dissemble,
      But follow where truth's voice is heard.

Come to us, mountain-dweller,
  Leader, wherever thou art;
    Skilled from thy cradle, a queller
      Of serpents, and sound to the heart!

Modest and mighty and tender;
  Man of an iron mold;
    Honest, fine-grained, our defender; —
      American-souled!

THE NAME OF WASHINGTON

[Read before the Sons of the Revolution, New-York
February 22, 1887]

Sons of the youth and the truth of the nation,
   Ye that are met to remember the man
Whose valor gave birth to a people's salvation,
   Honor him now; set his name in the van.
      A nobleness to try for,
      A name to live and die for —
        The name of Washington.

Calmly his face shall look down through the ages —
   Sweet yet severe with a spirit of warning;
Charged with the wisdom of saints and of sages;
   Quick with the light of a life-giving morning.
      A majesty to try for,
      A name to live and die for —
        The name of Washington!

Though faction may rack us, or party divide us,
   And bitterness break the gold links of our story,

Our father and leader is ever beside us.
 Live, and forgive! But forget not the glory
  Of him whose height we try for,
  A name to live and die for —
   The name of Washington!

Still in his eyes shall be mirrored our fleeting
 Days, with the image of days long ended;
Still shall those eyes give, immortally, greeting
 Unto the souls from his spirit descended.
   His grandeur we will try for,
   His name we 'll live and die for —
    The name of Washington!

GRANT'S DIRGE

I

Ah, who shall sound the hero's funeral march?
And what shall be the music of his dirge?
No single voice may chant the Nation's grief,
No formal strain can give its woe relief.
The pent-up anguish of the loyal wife,
The sobs of those who, nearest in this life,
Still hold him closely in the life beyond; —
These first, with threnody of memories fond.
But look! Forth press a myriad mourners thronging,
With hearts that throb in sorrow's exaltation,
Moved by a strange, impassioned, hopeless longing
To serve him with their love's last ministration.
Make way! Make way, from wave-bound verge
     to verge
Of all our land, that this great multitude
With lamentation proud albeit subdued,
Deep murmuring like the ocean's mighty surge,
May pass beneath the heavens' triumphal arch!

II

What is the sound we hear?
Never the fall of a tear;
For grief repressed
In every breast
More honors the man we revere.
Rising from East and West,
There echoes afar or near —
From the cool, sad North and the burning South —
A sound long since grown dear,
When brave ranks faced the cannon's mouth
And died for a faith austere :
The tread of marching men,
A steady tramp of feet
That never flinched nor faltered when
The drums of duty beat.
With sable hats whose shade
Falls from the cord of gold
On every time-worn face ;
With tattered flags, in black enrolled,
Beneath whose folds they warred of old ;
Forward, firmly arrayed,
With a sombre, martial' grace ;

So the Grand Army moves
Commanded by the dead,
Following him whose name it loves,
Whose voice in life its footsteps led.

III

Those that in the combat perished,—
  Hostile shapes and forms of friends,—
Those we hated, those we cherished,
  Meet the pageant where it ends.
Flash of steel and tears forgiving
  Blend in splendor.   Hark, the knell!
Comrades ghostly join the living —
  Dreaming, chanting: "All is well."
They receive the General sleeping,
  Him of spirit pure and large:
Him they draw into their keeping
  Evermore, in faithful charge.

IV

Pass on, O steps, with your dead, sad note!
  For a people's homage is in the sound;

And the even tread, in measured rote,
  As a leader is laid beneath the ground,
    Rumors the hum of a pilgrim train
    That shall trample the earth as tramples
      the rain,
    Seeking the door of the hero's tomb,
    Seeking him where he lies low in the gloom,
    Paying him tribute of worker and mage,
    Through age on age!

v

Tall pine-tree on McGregor's height,
How didst thou grow to such a lofty bearing,
For song of bird or beat of breeze uncaring,
There where thy shadow touched the dying brow?
Were all thy sinewy fibres shaped aright?
Was there no flaw? With what mysterious daring
Didst thou put forth each murmuring, odorous
    bough
And trust it to the frail support of air?
We only know that thou art now supreme:
We know not how thou grewest so tall and fair.
So from the unnoticed, humble earth arose

The sturdy man whom we, bewailing, deem
Worthy the wondrous name fame's far voice blows.
And lo! his ancient foes
Rise up to praise the plan
Of modest grandeur, loyal trust,
And generous power from man to man,
That lifted him above the formless dust.
O heart by kindliness betrayed,
O noble spirit snared and strayed —
Unmatched, upright thou standest still
As that firm pine-tree rooted on the hill!

VI

No paragon was he,
But moulded in the rough
With every fault and scar
Ingrained, and plain for all to see:
Even as the rocks and mountains are,
Common perhaps, yet wrought of such true stuff
That common nature in his essence grew
To something which till then it never knew;
Ay, common as a vast, refreshing wind
That sweeps the continent, or as some star

Which, 'mid a million, shines out well-defined:
With honest soul on duty bent,
A servant-soldier, President;
Meekest when crowned with victory,
And greatest in adversity!

VII

A silent man whom, strangely, fate
Made doubly silent ere he died,
His speechless spirit rules us still;
And that deep spell of influence mute,
The majesty of dauntless will
That wielded hosts and saved the State,
Seems through the mist our spirits yet to thrill.
His heart is with us! From the root
Of toil and pain and brave endurance
Has sprung at last the perfect fruit,
The treasure of a rich assurance
That men who nobly work and live
A greater gift than life may give;
Yielding a promise for all time,
Which other men of newer date
Surely redeem in deeds sublime.

Forerunner of a valiant race,
His voiceless spirit still reminds us
Of ever-waiting, silent duty :
The bond of faith wherewith he binds us
Shall hold us ready hour by hour
To serve the sacred, guiding power
Whene'er it calls, where'er it finds us,
With loyalty that, like a folded flower,
Blooms at a touch in proud, full-circled beauty.

VIII

Like swelling river waves that strain,
Onward the people crowd
In serried, billowing train.
And those so slow to yield,
On many a hard-fought field,
Muster together
Like a dark cloud
In summer weather,
Whose threatening thunders suddenly are stilled,—
And all the world is filled
With smiling rest. Victory to him was pain,
Till he had won his enemies by love;
Had leashed the eagle and unloosed the dove;

Setting on war's red roll the argent seal of peace.
So here they form their solid ranks again,
But in no mood of hatred or disdain.
They say: "Thou who art fallen at last,
Beleaguered stealthily, o'ercome by death,
Thy conqueror now shall be magnanimous
Even as thou wast to us.
But not for thee can we blot out the past:
We would not, if we might, forget thy last
Great act of war, that with a gentle hand
Brought back our hearts unto the mighty mother,
For whose defence and honor armed we stand.
We hail thee brother,
And so salute thy name with holy breath!"

IX

    Land of the hurricane!
Land of the avalanche!
Land of tempest and rain;
Of the Southern sun and of frozen peaks;
Stretching from main to main;—
Land of the cypress-glooms;
Land of devouring looms;
Land of the forest and ranch;—

Hush every sound to-day
Save the burden of swarms that assemble
Their reverence dear to pay
Unto him who saved us all!
Ye masses that mourn with bended head,
Beneath whose feet the ground doth tremble
With weight of woe and a sacred dread —
Lift up the pall
That to us shall remain as a warrior's banner!
Gaze once more on the fast closed eyes;
Mark once the mouth that never speaks;
Think of the man and his quiet manner:
Weep if you will; then go your way;
But remember his face as it looks to the skies,
And the dumb appeal wherewith it seeks
To lead us on, as one should say, "Arise —
Go forth to meet your country's noblest day!"

x

Ah, who shall sound the hero's funeral march?
  And what shall be the music of his dirge?
  Let generations sing, as they emerge
And pass beneath the heavens' trumphal arch!

BATTLE DAYS

I

Veteran memories rally to muster
  Here at the call of the old battle days:
Cavalry clatter and cannon's hoarse bluster:
  All the wild whirl of the fight's broken
    maze :
Clangor of bugle and flashing of sabre,
  Smoke-stifled flags and the howl of the shell,
With earth for a rest place and death for a
    neighbor,
    And dreams of a charge and the deep rebel
      yell.
Stern was our task in the field where the reap-
    ing
    Spared the ripe harvest, but laid our men
      low :
Grim was the sorrow that held us from weeping :
  Awful the rush of the strife's ebb and flow.

Swift came the silence—our enemy hiding
  Sudden retreat in the cloud-muffled night:
Swift as a hawk-pounce our hill-and-dale riding;
    Hundreds on hundreds we caught in their
      flight!
Hard and incessant the danger and trial,
  Laid on our squadrons, that gladly bore all,
Scorning to meet with delay or denial
    The summons that rang in the battle-days'
      call!

II

Wild days that woke to glory or despair,
  And smote the coward soul with sudden
    shame,
But unto those whose hearts were bold to dare
  All things for honor brought eternal
    fame:—
        Lost days, undying days!
        With undiminished rays
        Here now on us look down,
        Illumining our crown
Of leaves memorial, wet with tender dew
  For those who nobly died

In fierce self-sacrifice of service true,
  Rapt in pure fire of life-disdaining pride;
Men of this soil, who stood
  Firm for their country's good,
From night to night, from sun to sun,
  Till o'er the living and the slain
A woful dawn that streamed with rain
  Wept for their victory dearly won.

III

Days of the future, prophetic days,—
  Silence engulfs the roar of war;
Yet, through all coming years, repeat the
    praise
    Of those leal comrades brave, who come no
      more!
And when our voices cease,
  Long, long renew the chant, the anthem
      proud,
Which, echoing clear and loud
  Through templed aisles of peace,
Like blended tumults of a joyous chime,
Shall tell their valor to a later time.

Shine on this field; and in the eyes of men
Rekindle, if the need shall come again,
That answering light that springs
In beaconing splendor from the soul, and
        brings
Promise of faith well kept and deed sublime!

KEENAN'S CHARGE

[CHANCELLORSVILLE, MAY, 1863]

I

The sun had set;
The leaves with dew were wet:
Down fell a bloody dusk
On the woods, that second of May,
Where Stonewall's corps, like a beast of prey,
Tore through, with angry tusk.

" They 've trapped us, boys!"—
Rose from our flank a voice.
With a rush of steel and smoke
On came the rebels straight,
Eager as love and wild as hate;
And our line reeled and broke;

Broke and fled.
No one stayed—but the dead!

With curses, shrieks, and cries,
Horses and wagons and men
Tumbled back through the shuddering glen,
And above us the fading skies.

There 's one hope, still —
Those batteries parked on the hill!
" Battery, wheel!" ('mid the roar)
" Pass pieces; fix prolonge to fire
Retiring. Trot!" In the panic dire
A bugle rings " Trot " — and no more.

The horses plunged,
The cannon lurched and lunged,
To join the hopeless rout.
But suddenly rode a form
Calmly in front of the human storm,
With a stern, commanding shout:

" Align those guns!"
(We knew it was Pleasonton's.)
The cannoneers bent to obey,
And worked with a will at his word:
And the black guns moved as if *they* had heard.
But ah, the dread delay!

" To wait is crime ;
    O God, for ten minutes' time ! "
    The General looked around.
    There Keenan sat, like a stone,
    With his three hundred horse alone,
    Less shaken than the ground.

" Major, your men ? "
" Are soldiers, General."   " Then,
    Charge, Major !   Do your best :
    Hold the enemy back, at all cost,
    Till my guns are placed ; — else the army is lost.
    You die to save the rest ! "

                    II

    By the shrouded gleam of the western skies,
    Brave Keenan looked into Pleasonton's eyes
    For an instant — clear, and cool, and still ;
    Then, with a smile, he said : " I will."

" Cavalry, charge ! "   Not a man of them shrank.
    Their sharp, full cheer, from rank on rank,
    Rose joyously, with a willing breath —
    Rose like a greeting hail to death.

Then forward they sprang, and spurred and
    clashed;
Shouted the officers, crimson-sash'd;
Rode well the men, each brave as his fellow,
In their faded coats of the blue and yellow;
And above in the air, with an instinct true,
Like a bird of war their pennon flew.

With clank of scabbards and thunder of steeds,
And blades that shine like sunlit reeds,
And strong brown faces bravely pale
For fear their proud attempt shall fail,
Three hundred Pennsylvanians close
On twice ten thousand gallant foes.

Line after line the troopers came
To the edge of the wood that was ring'd with
    flame;
Rode in and sabred and shot — and fell;
Nor came one back his wounds to tell.
And full in the midst rose Keenan, tall,
In the gloom like a martyr awaiting his fall,
While the circle-stroke of his sabre, swung
'Round his head, like a halo there, luminous
    hung.

Line after line, aye, whole platoons,
Struck dead in their saddles, of brave dragoons
By the maddened horses were onward borne
And into the vortex flung, trampled and torn;
As Keenan fought with his men, side by side.

So they rode, till there were no more to ride.

But over them, lying there shattered and mute,
What deep echo rolls? — 'T is a death-salute,
From the cannon in place; for heroes, you braved
Your fate not in vain: the army was saved!

Over them now — year following year —
Over their graves the pine-cones fall,
And the whip-poor-will chants his spectre-call;
But they stir not again: they raise no cheer:
They have ceased. But their glory shall never
    cease,
Nor their light be quenched in the light of peace.
The rush of their charge is resounding still
That saved the army at Chancellorsville.

"There, on the left!" said the colonel: the battle
　had shuddered and faded away,
Wraith of a fiery enchantment that left only
　ashes and blood-sprinkled clay —
"Ride to the left and examine that ridge, where
　the enemy's sharpshooters stood.
Lord, how they picked off our men, from the
　treacherous vantage-ground of the wood!
But for their bullets, I 'll bet, my batteries sent
　them something as good.
Go and explore, and report to me then, and tell
　me how many we killed.
Never a wink shall I sleep till I know our ven-
　geance was duly fulfilled."

Fiercely the orderly rode down the slope of the
　corn-field — scarred and forlorn,
Rutted by violent wheels, and scathed by the
　shot that had plowed it in scorn;

Fiercely, and burning with wrath for the sight
    of his comrades crushed at a blow,
Flung in broken shapes on the ground like
    ruined memorials of woe:
These were the men whom at daybreak he knew,
    but never again could know.
Thence to the ridge, where roots outthrust, and
    twisted branches of trees
Clutched the hill like clawing lions, firm their
    prey to seize.

" What 's your report ? "— and the grim colonel
    smiled when the orderly came back at last.
Strangely the soldier paused : " Well, they were
    punished." And strange his face, aghast.
" Yes, our fire told on them ; knocked over fifty —
    laid out in line of parade.
Brave fellows, colonel, to stay as they did ! But
    one I 'most wish had n't stayed.
Mortally wounded, he 'd torn off his knapsack ;
    and then at the end he prayed —
Easy to see, by his hands that were clasped ;
    and the dull, dead fingers yet held
This little letter—his wife's—from the knapsack.
    A pity those woods were shelled ! "

Silent the orderly, watching with tears in his eyes
    as his officer scanned
Four short pages of writing. "What's this, about
    'Marthy Virginia's hand'?"
Swift from his honeymoon he, the dead soldier,
    had gone from his bride to the strife;
Never they met again, but she had written him,
    telling of that new life,
Born in the daughter, that bound her still closer
    and closer to him as his wife.
Laying her baby's hand down on the letter,
    around it she traced a rude line;
"If you would kiss the baby," she wrote, "you
    must kiss this outline of mine."

There was the shape of the hand on the page,
    with the small, chubby fingers outspread.
"Marthy Virginia's hand, for her pa,"—so the
    words on the little palm said.
Never a wink slept the colonel that night, for
    the vengeance so blindly fulfilled;
Never again woke the old battle-glow when the
    bullets their death-note shrilled.
Long ago ended the struggle, in union of
    brotherhood happily stilled;

Yet from that field of Antietam, in warning and
    token of love's command,
See! there is lifted the hand of a baby — Marthy
    Virginia's hand!

GETTYSBURG: A BATTLE ODE

I

Victors, living, with laureled brow,
   And you that sleep beneath the sward!
Your song was poured from cannon throats:
It rang in deep-tongued bugle-notes:
Your triumph came; you won your crown,
The grandeur of a world's renown.
     But, in our later lays,
     Full freighted with your praise,
Fair memory harbors those whose lives, laid down
   In gallant faith and generous heat,
    Gained only sharp defeat.
All are at peace, who once so fiercely warred:
Brother and brother, now, we chant a common chord.

II

For, if we say God wills,
Shall we then idly deny Him
Care of each host in the fight?

His thunder was here in the hills
When the guns were loud in July;
And the flash of the musketry's light
Was sped by a ray from God's eye.
In its good and its evil the scheme
Was framed with omnipotent hand,
Though the battle of men was a dream
That they could but half understand.
Can the purpose of God pass by him?
Nay; it was sure, and was wrought
Under inscrutable powers:
Bravely the two armies fought
And left the land, that was greater than they, still
theirs and ours!

III

Lucid, pure, and calm and blameless
Dawned on Gettysburg the day
That should make the spot, once fameless,
Known to nations far away.
Birds were caroling, and farmers
Gladdened o'er their garnered hay,
When the clank of gathering armors

Broke the morning's peaceful sway;
And the living lines of foemen
    Drawn o'er pasture, brook, and hill,
Formed in figures weird of omen
    That should work with mystic will
Measures of a direful magic —
    Shattering, maiming — and should fill
Glades and gorges with a tragic
    Madness of desire to kill.
Skirmishers flung lightly forward
    Moved like scythemen skilled to sweep
Westward o'er the field and nor'ward,
    Death's first harvest there to reap.
You would say the soft, white smoke-puffs
    Were but languid clouds asleep,
Here on meadows, there on oak-bluffs,
    Fallen foam of Heaven's blue deep.
Yet that blossom-white outbreaking
    Smoke wove soon a martyr's shroud.
Reynolds fell, with soul unquaking,
    Ardent-eyed and open-browed:
Noble men in humbler raiment
    Fell where shot their graves had plowed,
Dying not for paltry payment:
    Proud of home, of honor proud.

IV

Mute Seminary there,
Filled once with resonant hymn and prayer,
How your meek walls and windows shuddered
then!
Though Doubleday stemmed the flood,
McPherson's Wood and Willoughby's Run
Saw ere the set of sun
The light of the gospel of blood.
And, on the morrow again,
Loud the unholy psalm of battle
Burst from the tortured Devil's Den,
In cries of men and musketry rattle
Mixed with the helpless bellow of cattle
Torn by artillery, down in the glen;
While, hurtling through the branches
Of the orchard by the road,
Where Sickles and Birney were walled with steel,
Shot fiery avalanches
That shivered hope and made the sturdiest reel.
Yet peach-bloom bright as April saw
Blushed there anew, in blood that flowed
O'er faces white with death-dealt awe;
And ruddy flowers of warfare grew,

Though withering winds as of the desert blew,
 Far at the right while Ewell and Early,
  Plunging at Slocum and Wadsworth and
   Greene,
 Thundered in onslaught consummate and surly;
 Till trembling nightfall crept between
And whispered of rest from the heat of the
  whelming strife.
  But unto those forsaken of life
  What has the night to say ?
 Silent beneath the moony sky,
 Crushed in a costly dew they lie:
 Deaf to plaint or pæan, they :—
 Freed from Earth's dull tyranny.

     v

Wordless the night-wind, funereal plumes of the
  tree-tops swaying—
 Writhing and nodding anon at the beck of the
  unseen breeze!
Yet its voice ever a murmur resumes, as of multitudes praying :
 Liturgies lost in a moan like the mourning of
  far-away seas.

May then those spirits, set free, a celestial coun-
cil obeying,
  Move in this rustling whisper here thro' the
  dark, shaken trees? —
Souls that are voices alone to us, now, yet linger,
returning
  Thrilled with a sweet reconcilement and fervid
  with speechless desire?
Sundered in warfare, immortal they meet now with
wonder and yearning,
  Dwelling together united, a rapt, invisible choir:
Hearken! They wail for the living, whose passion
of battle, yet burning,
Sears and enfolds them in coils, and consumes,
  like a serpent of fire!

VI

Men of New Hampshire, Pennsylvanians,
  Maine men, firm as the rock's rough ledge!
Swift Mississippians, lithe Carolinians
  Bursting over the battle's edge!
Bold Indiana men; gallant Virginians;
  Jersey and Georgia legions clashing; —

Pick of Connecticut; quick Vermonters;
　Louisianians, madly dashing; —
And, swooping still to fresh encounters,
　New-York myriads, whirlwind-led! —
All your furious forces, meeting,
　Torn, entangled, and shifting place,
Blend like wings of eagles beating
　Airy abysses, in angry embrace.
Here in the midmost struggle combining —
　Flags immingled and weapons crossed —
Still in union your States troop shining:
　Never a star from the lustre is lost!

VII

Once more the sun deploys his rays:
Third in the trilogy of battle-days
　The awful Friday comes:
　　A day of dread,
That should have moved with slow, averted
　　　head
　　And muffled feet,
Knowing what streams of pure blood shed,

What broken hearts and wounded lives must
  meet
 Its pitiless tread.
At dawn, like monster mastiffs baying,
Federal cannon, with a din affraying,
Roused the old Stonewall brigade,
That, eagerly and undismayed,
Charged amain, to be repelled
 After four hours' bitter fighting,
 Forth and back, with bayonets biting;
Where in after years, the wood —
Flayed and bullet-riddled — stood
A presence ghostly, grim and stark,
 With trees all withered, wasted, gray,
 The place of combat night and day
Like marshaled skeletons to mark.
Anon, a lull: the troops are spelled.
  No sound of guns or drums
  Disturbs the air.
Only the insect-chorus faintly hums,
 Chirping around the patient, sleepless dead
Scattered, or fallen in heaps all wildly spread;
Forgotten fragments left in hurried flight;
 Forms that, a few hours since, were human
  creatures,

Now blasted of their features,
Or stamped with blank despair;
Or with dumb faces smiling as for gladness,
Though stricken by utter blight
Of motionless, inert, and hopeless sadness.
Fear you the naked horrors of a war?
Then cherish peace, and take up arms no more.
For, if you fight, you must
Behold your brothers' dust
Unpityingly ground down
And mixed with blood and powder,
To write the annals of renown
That make a nation prouder!

VIII

All is quiet till one o'clock;
Then the hundred and fifty guns,
Metal loaded with metal in tons,
Massed by Lee, send out their shock.
And, with a movement magnificent,
Pickett, the golden-haired leader,
Thousands and thousands flings onward, as if he sent
Merely a meek interceder.

Steadily sure his division advances,
Gay as the light on its weapons that dances.
Agonized screams of the shell
The doom that it carries foretell:
Rifle-balls whistle, like sea-birds singing;
Limbs are severed, and souls set winging;
Yet Pickett's warriors never waver.
Show me in all the world anything braver
Than the bold sweep of his fearless battalions,
Three half-miles over ground unsheltered
Up to the cannon, where regiments weltered
Prone in the batteries' blast that raked
Swaths of men and, flame-tongued, drank
Their blood with eager thirst unslaked.
Armistead, Kemper, and Pettigrew
Rush on the Union men, rank against rank,
Planting their battle-flags high on the crest.
Pause not the soldiers, nor dream they of rest,
Till they fall with their enemy's guns at the
breast
And the shriek in their ears of the wounded ar-
tillery stallions.
So Pickett charged, a man indued
With knightly power to lead a multitude
And bring to fame the scarred surviving few.

IX

In vain the mighty endeavor;
In vain the immortal valor;
In vain the insurgent life outpoured!
Faltered the column, spent with shot and
    sword;
Its bright hope blanched with sudden pallor;
While Hancock's trefoil bloomed in triple fame.
He chose the field; he saved the second day;
    And, honoring here his glorious name,
Again his phalanx held victorious sway.
Meade's line stood firm, and volley on volley
    roared
Triumphant Union, soon to be restored,
Strong to defy all foes and fears forever.
    The Ridge was wreathed with angry fire
    As flames rise round a martyr's stake;
For many a hero on that pyre
    Was offered for our dear land's sake,
    What time in heaven the gray clouds flew
    To mingle with the deathless blue;
    While here, below, the blue and gray
    Melted minglingly away,
Mirroring heaven, to make another day.

And we, who are Americans, we pray
  The splendor of strength that Gettysburg
    knew
May light the long generations with glorious ray,
  And keep us undyingly true!

X

Dear are the dead we weep for;
  Dear are the strong hearts broken!
Proudly their memory we keep for
  Our help and hope; a token
Of sacred thought too deep for
  Words that leave it unspoken.
All that we know of fairest,
  All that we have of meetest,
Here we lay down for the rarest
  Doers whose souls rose fleetest
And in their homes of air rest,
  Ranked with the truest and sweetest.
Days, with fiery-hearted, bold advances;
  Nights in dim and shadowy, swift retreat;
Rains that rush with bright, embattled lances;
  Thunder, booming round your stirless feet; —
Winds that set the orchard with sweet fancies
  All abloom, or ripple the ripening wheat;

Moonlight, starlight, on your mute graves falling;
    Dew, distilled as tears unbidden flow; —
Dust of drought in drifts and layers crawling;
    Lulling dreams of softly whispering snow;
Happy birds, from leafy coverts calling; —
    These go on, yet none of these you know:
      Hearing not our human voices
      Speaking to you all in vain,
      Nor the psalm of a land that rejoices,
Ringing from churches and cities and foundries a
      mighty refrain!
But we, and the sun and the birds, and the breezes
      that blow
When tempests are striving and lightnings of
      heaven are spent,
      With one consent
      Make unto them
      Who died for us eternal requiem.

XI

    Lovely to look on, O South,
      No longer stately-scornful
    But beautiful still in pride,
Our hearts go out to you as toward a bride!
    Garmented soft in white,

Haughty, and yet how love-imbuing and tender!
You stand before us with your gently mournful
Memory-haunted eyes and flower-like mouth,
  Where clinging thoughts — as bees a-cluster
  Murmur through the leafy gloom,
    Musical in monotone —
  Whisper sadly. Yet a lustre
  As of glowing gold-gray light
    Shines upon the orient bloom,
    Sweet with orange-blossoms, thrown
  Round the jasmine-starred, deep night
  Crowning with dark hair your brow.
  Ruthless, once, we came to slay,
    And you met us then with hate.
  Rough was the wooing of war: we won you,
    Won you at last, though late!
      Dear South, to-day,
  As our country's altar made us
    One forever, so we vow
  Unto yours our love to render:
  Strength with strength we here endow,
  And we make your honor ours.
Happiness and hope shall sun you:
All the wiles that half betrayed us
  Vanish from us like spent showers.

XII

Two hostile bullets in mid-air
 Together shocked,
 And swift were locked
Forever in a firm embrace.
Then let us men have so much grace
 To take the bullets' place,
 And learn that we are held
  By laws that weld
  Our hearts together!
As once we battled hand to hand,
 So hand in hand to-day we stand,
  Sworn to each other,
  Brother and brother,
In storm and mist, or calm, translucent weather:
And Gettysburg's guns, with their death-giving
  roar,
Echoed from ocean to ocean, shall pour
 Quickening life to the nation's core;
  Filling our minds again
 With the spirit of those who wrought in the
  Field of the Flower of Men!

NOTES

¹ *Bride Brook.*—The colony of New London (now part of Connecticut) was founded by John Winthrop, Jr., under the jurisdiction of Massachusetts. One of the boundary lines was a stream flowing into Long Island Sound, between the present city of New London and the Connecticut River. In the snowy winter of 1646, Jonathan Rudd, who dwelt in the settlement of Saybrook Fort, at the mouth of the Connecticut, sent for Winthrop to celebrate a marriage between himself and a certain " Mary " of Saybrook, whose last name has been lost. Winthrop performed the ceremony on the frozen surface of the streamlet, the farthest limit of his magistracy; and thereupon bestowed the name " Bride Brook," which it still bears.

² *The Bride of War.*—Jemima Warner, a Pennsylvania woman, was the wife of one of Morgan's riflemen. She marched with the expedition ; and, when her husband perished of cold and exhaustion, she took his rifle and equipments and herself carried them to Quebec, where she delivered them to Arnold as a token of her husband's sacrifice, and proof that he was not a deserter.

Colonel Enos of Connecticut abandoned the column while it was struggling through the Dead River region, with his whole force, the rear-guard, numbering eight

hundred men.   But for this defection Arnold might
have triumphed in his assault on Quebec.   It is a curious circumstance that, with this traitor at the rear, and
with Benedict Arnold at its head, the little army also
counted in its ranks Aaron Burr, whose treason was to
ripen after the war ended.

[3] *The Sword Dham.*—Antar, the Bedouin poet-hero,
was chief of the tribe of Ghaylib.

[4] *The Name of Washington.*— Read before the Sons
of the Revolution, New-York, February 22, 1887, and
adopted as the poem of the Society.

[5] *Marthy Virginia's Hand.*— This was an actual
incident in the experience of the late Colonel (formerly
Captain) Albert J. Munroe, of the Third Rhode Island
Artillery, a gallant officer, gentle and brave as well in
peace as in war.

[6] *Gettysburg: A Battle Ode.*— Written for the Society of the Army of the Potomac, and read at its
re-union with Confederate survivors on the field of
Gettysburg, July 3, 1888, the Twenty-Fifth Anniversary
of the Battle.